Faith and reality

Faith and reality

Wolfhart Pannenberg

Translated by John Maxwell

The Westminster Press · Philadelphia

First published in German, under the title
*Glaube und Wirklichkeit. Kleine Beiträge zum
christlichen Denken,* by Chr. Kaiser Verlag of
Munich, Federal Republic of Germany, 1975

First published in this translation in Great Britain
in 1977 by Search Press, London, and in the
United States of America by The Westminster
Press of Philadelphia, Pa.

Published by The Westminster Press®
Philadelphia, Pennsylvania

PRINTED IN THE UNITED STATES OF AMERICA

Library of Congress Cataloging in Publication Data

Pannenberg, Wolfhart, 1928–
  Faith and reality.

  Translation of Glaube und Wirklichkeit.
  1. Theology — Addresses, essays, lectures. I. Title.
BR85.P2613 1977   230   77-682
ISBN 0-664-24755-5

Contents

Foreword

Most of the lectures and essays in this volume are addressed not to professional theologians but to a wider public. Nevertheless the general theme, which may be described as the confrontation of the Christian tradition of faith with the contemporary experience of reality, required the inclusion of a few more specialized studies.

The first essay announces the theme of the book: the connexion between the God-question and our understanding of reality. The second article, seven years older than the first, is intended to show how the scriptural understanding of reality was influenced by Israel's experience of God. The provenance of my theological interest in the relation between understanding God and understanding reality is Old Testament exegesis as presented by my teacher Gerhard von Rad. This is especially evident in the historico-theological tenor of my work. In recent years I have looked more closely at the implications of modern science for understanding of the world; I have incorporated my findings in an explicitly historical interpretation of reality. That is clear from the first essay and from the third, which deals most extensively with systematic concept-formation in an attempted resolution of the complex of problems raised by the natural sciences. The association of the theory of evolution with a reading of nature as history is of course an implicit topic here. The fourth contribution moves from the general phenomenon of life to the question of man and his destiny, and proceeds eventually to the topic of human history, which is taken up and extended in the subsequent articles.

These four essays were written in the early nineteen-sixties, during the first stage of my evolving conception of the theology of history. In simplifying my theses for the larger audience of

Evangelical scholars, I emphasized most of all something that I already stressed heavily in that phase: the grounding of faith in knowledge gained from historical experience. That emphasis was primarily directed against an irrationally subjective but widespread idea: namely, that the essentials of faith originate in the decision of faith, and only thus are perceived by the believer, or become comprehensible and convincing for him. It was also directed against a faith which stressed authority, and thus adhered to the same subjective belief. The error there is to see the substance of faith as something apart from rational scrutiny and demanding as a precondition of understanding an act of subjection (which it calls obedient faith) to the authority of the kerygma or the revelation to which Scripture testifies; an authority represented though not demonstrable as the word of God. That kind of faith in authority has now succumbed to subjectivism, precisely because such unprovable appeals to authority can be accepted only by irrational decision.

In spite of the foregoing, I still believe that Jewish and Christian faith grew out of historical experiences and reflection on their implications, and that grasp and scrutiny of them now demand before all else acquaintance with their content, and are therefore a matter of historical knowledge and insight into its scope. But I now assess the degree of theoretical certainty attainable in that way more subtly than might be imagined from some of my past formulations. In the meantime an insight available then (though not grasped in all its implications) has become increasingly important: namely, the notion that the provisional nature and consequent pluralism of our knowledge of God's revelation in history themselves form part of the essential structure of that same revelation.

The eighth essay was my first attempt to apply to the history of Christianity, and especially to modern history, a conception of the theology of history obtained from Scripture and developed in the light of the modern approach to theological and philosophical problems. That attempt is continued in the penultimate essay, on the relation between political universalism and nationalism, which is central to the foregoing task. That theme leads to the final contribution, on ethics. I have been concerned ever since with a theological interpretation of the history of Christianity and its world. Whereas here nationalism appears as an ideology wholly alien to Christian supranationalism, I have in the meantime reached the conclusion that in the historical world of Christianity itself nationalism is mediated by Christian impulses. Particularly in its medieval beginnings, but also in the England of the seventeenth century, in North America, and in the European states of the modern era, nationalism appears as a form of faith in election. That faith, in view of the decay of the political unity of Christianity as the new people of God, transferred the election of the people of Israel (by analogy) to a specific nation. The theological motivation of the nationalisms which originated within Christian civilization naturally demands critical scrutiny. It certainly does not imply any change in my judgment of the opposition between nationalism and Christian universalism. In that respect my ideas have not changed.

The penultimate essay was given as a lecture to the Evangelical Study Circle of the Christian Democratic Union (CDU) in the Federal Republic in 1965, and was intended as a warning to those flirting with nationalistic tendencies. It ends with a then topical reference; to the German Frontier question; the problem, that is of the East–West border between the present territory of the two German States and Poland, the Soviet Union, and so on. The substance of what I was saying no longer seems in any way strange, but is largely accepted as part of political reality. In 1965 on the other hand it awakened strong reactions and even a flood of anonymous threats. I have left the relevant sentences as they were written.

WOLFHART PANNENBERG

I Our life in God's hands?

Has the reality of our life anything at all to do with God? This is a question that has become distressingly urgent for Christians today. If there were indeed no connexion between our lives and God, then everything that we have to say about God would be in vain. What would be the purpose of proclaiming God as our creator and the one who keeps us in existence or as the Lord of history, if our lives were led entirely without regard to God's will or activity? It is an empirical fact that more and more people are finding the traditional language of religion difficult or even impossible to accept nowadays. It seems to them that life can function perfectly well without God. This must, of course, be connected with the fact that the very word 'God' is playing a decreasingly important part in everyday speech. The idea of God is no longer the absolute and indispensable foundation of our life and behaviour in this world. If it plays any part at all, it is often only to disturb or even obstruct our functioning and to inhibit our full enjoyment of life. Many people strongly object to this type of experience.

It is, in this context, valuable to consider Christian reactions to this loss of reality in what we say about God. The simplest and most instinctive reaction is, of course, to barricade oneself against any changes in society that threaten faith and to seek refuge in the traditional language and thought-patterns of Christianity. This attitude can, however, only succeed as long as the present changes which are apparently so unfavourable to Christianity are no more than passing phenomena. But everything points to the fact that the change taking place in the present century is absolutely fundamental, will be very long-lasting and will ultimately result in man's becoming completely free of all dependence on traditional patterns of religious thought. He is moving quite rapidly towards a radically new understanding of reality, and Christian believers and theologians must adapt themselves to this new way of thinking if they want to prevent any further loss of reality in what they have to say about God. It is for this reason that some of the most perceptive Christian thinkers have tended to regard man's movement away from the traditional Christian idea of God as a problem of religious language and to say that it is not God himself who has become superfluous, but rather a traditional way of understanding God. They claim that the death-of-God theology marked the end of our earlier and antiquated understanding of God and that this was wrongly equated with the end of the reality of God himself. In making this claim, however, it is important to be able to distinguish between the reality of God and man's theistic idea of a spiritual being as the first cause of the world, and then to show how, in a new sense, the reality of our life cannot be understood without God. I will therefore attempt here to throw a little more light on the gulf that separates our present-day understanding of the situation in which man finds himself in the world from the earlier, traditional Christian view of life.

Let us first consider our understanding of nature. Mediaeval man found the processes of nature incomprehensible unless he presupposed a first cause, which was in turn unchangeable since, if it had been changeable, there must have been a cause for its changeability. The conclusion that was drawn from the unchangeable nature of this first cause was that it must have been a spiritual reality and this led inevitably to the idea of a personal God. This first cause did not, however, necessarily have to be regarded as a first beginning of all natural processes, though there was at least a need for a first sustaining cause which would prevent the natural processes from becoming less effective. There was a conviction that every movement required continuous impulses if it was not to come to a halt. This need for the acceptance of ceaseless divine activity without which all movement in nature would be bound to end eventually became superfluous when the principle of inertia was introduced in the seventeenth century. This idea played an immensely important part in the process by which God was elimi-

nated from nature. According to the law of inertia, every moved
body tended to persist of its own accord in its movement so long
as it was not retarded or accelerated in that movement by outside influences. This seventeenth-century law is clearly important for us here because its acceptance implied that there was
no further need to explain the continuously moving process of
nature by recourse to an infinite and all-embracing divine
power; the movement of nature continued of its own accord.
The principle of inertia, then, was the first and perhaps most
striking example of how man's understanding of the world became dissociated from traditional religious presuppositions,
and how the idea began to develop that the world could be
understood purely in relation to itself.

Let us now consider another example of the same principle—
that of the origin of life. According to the very early Christian
understanding of the world, life—and especially human life—
was entirely dependent on the activity of the Spirit of God,
with the result that all creatures were filled with terror when
God hid his face: 'When thou takest away their breath, they
die and return to their dust; when thou sendest forth thy
Spirit, they are created and thou renewest the face of the
ground' (Ps 104.29–30). The Spirit of God, which animated all
living beings, was, according to this early view, identical with
the fertile wind which caused the surface of the earth to become
green in springtime. The origin of life was thus seen in an entirely transcendent light. Later, during the Middle Ages, the
development of the idea that the soul was the animating principle of the body conferred a certain independence on the creature, but the soul was still believed to have originated in God.
Modern, scientifically-orientated man, however, traces the
origin of all living organisms back to living matter and regards
the living cell as the principle of all expressions of life. He claims
that there is no need to have recourse to the idea of a soul animating the body in order to explain the processes of life.

There is a clear parallel here with the law of inertia. In both
cases, life is understood in terms of itself. In our first example,
the movement of life is seen as continuing of its own accord and,
in this second example, both the reproductive processes of life

in the individual organism and the reproduction and evolution of entire species are seen as processes in the development of the living cell. In the present century we may even have reached the culminating point of this view of life, namely that living cells were originally produced from inorganic matter. What is certain is that there is no place in this view of the origin and development of life for the traditional divine origin of life.

Our third and last example is taken from man's changing understanding of history. According to the traditional Christian view, history was above all the sphere in which God's providence and government of the world manifested themselves, man being regarded as the object of God's decisions. It was God who apportioned times of prosperity and times of suffering to the individual and who determined the hour of his death. God also determined the whole course of human history, the fate of nations and the outcome of all wars. The Book of Proverbs provides many instances of the clear distinction that was made in this early view between man's plans and God's providence: 'A man's mind plans his way, but the Lord directs his steps' (Prov 16.9); 'The horse is made ready for the day of battle, but the victory belongs to the Lord' (21.31); and so on. According to this view, then, man shares in his activity in history, but his short-sighted plans are directed towards ends which are quite different from those pursued by God, who only makes use of man and his activity to achieve his aims.

According to the modern understanding of human history, man is given a central position. This does not mean that man's actions always achieve the results that he plans. On the contrary, they often result in something quite different, but the cause of this difference is not now sought in God and his counsel, but in man's own failure. Modern man has undoubtedly succeeded in gaining increasing control over the conditions governing his existence. This is particularly true of the natural conditions of his environment, which he has learnt to put at his service and to make subservient to his own needs and aims to an extraordinary degree by means of constantly developing technology. He has, of course, been less strikingly successful in controlling the social conditions of his life. The rather naïvely optimistic hope of the immediately preceding centuries in the apparently natural progress of human civilization has lost its impetus in a century which has experienced the most destructive and terrible wars in modern history. All the same, it would seem to be impossible for man to give up trying to achieve a rational regulation of the natural and social conditions governing his life on earth.

It is in fact still very uncertain whether man will ever succeed in gaining rational control of these conditions while at the same time preserving the individual freedom that has come about as the result of democratic striving in the West. It would seem to be almost as difficult as squaring the circle. The Old Testament proverbs would appear therefore still to be true: in other words, man may plan, but the outcome of his plans is not in his hands. This would seem to apply both to man in society and to the individual. Not only the failure, but the success of our plans would appear to be indissolubly linked to the ultimate mystery which penetrates and surrounds everything that we do, transcends all our human experience, and in the end decides whether we are to succeed or to fail. Nowadays, we may have many reservations concerning any attempt to trace the course of historical events back to a divine reality guiding them, but it is undeniably true that history always transcends the particular aims of each individual. The actions of many different individuals give rise to interconnexions in the meaning of the events which those individuals can themselves at most only partly foresee and by which they are often unpredictably surprised. These interconnexions between various events which transcend the individuals who have been responsible for the events themselves are not, it must be stressed, simply the work of active men. History rises above the model of the process which operates of its own accord.

This modern tendency by which man has come to occupy a central and controlling place in history has, however, made it very difficult to describe the processes of human life in detail. These processes can only be defined in general and the particular life-history of the individual organism has to be left aside. On the other hand, anything that is said about the life-processes within the individual cell is bound to overlook the essential reality that applies to life in general: namely, that individual life can be fulfilled only if it transcends itself in time and in space. Even in its search for food, the living organism is entering into a relationship with a future which will bring about an irreversible change in its own being, and thus at the same time into an environment which has hitherto only existed outside itself. This openness to the world beyond itself exposes the organism to the historicity of its own unique life experience. This historical reality is in fact in the most radical sense the very life itself of the organism and can never be adequately described simply in terms of the functioning of living cells. The essential miracle of life itself is to be found in the actual individual history and all general biological statements can, when this miracle is considered, be left out of account.

The same can be applied to the process of nature in general. There is a good deal of evidence to support the theory that the world as a whole forms part of a unique and unrepeatable process, in which each individual event is also unique insofar as the form that the particular event takes is conditioned by constantly outdated forms. The natural process can only be described if this unique aspect is overlooked, yet it is, of course, precisely this unique and unrepeatable quality that constitutes the real mystery of the natural process. Real movement can never provide us with a pure example of inertia because it is always determined by very complex changes in state. On the other hand, the constant and unchanging nature of forms and laws also becomes very problematical when seen in the light of this unique quality of the natural process which, in our superficial understanding, we so often and so easily regard as an inherent part of the law of nature.

We may therefore conclude that, because of the historicity of this unique process of life, we no longer believe that nature, life and history can ever be described in detail as processes that take place simply of their own accord. At the same time, however, this new insight can also make us conscious of the miracle of nature, life and history. Would it perhaps be possible to express this idea as a newly discovered trust that our life and his-

tory is in God's hands? Not if we mean by this that God's activity should be regarded as competing with man's activity, the
evolutionary processes of life and the laws of nature. When,
however, we learn to see this all-embracing and transcendent
miracle of nature, life and history as the sign of God's presence
among us it will once again become meaningful to speak about
God whenever we wish to speak about the real meaning of our
life and our history.

II The biblical
understanding of reality

It is very difficult to define the term 'reality'. This difficulty is, of course, connected with the fact that the word has such a wide-ranging meaning. We apply the word to almost everything with which we are concerned in some way and, what is more, everything regarded as an entirety. 'Reality' has therefore come to mean almost the same as 'the whole of being', though it does, however, mean more than the mere presence of things. Whenever we say that something is a reality for us, what we mean is that something essential is involved, something that is really important and concerns our life as a whole. According to Hegel, reality is the unity of essential being and existence; it is real insofar as it is effective, can be experienced and is directly related to the whole. We may therefore say that reality is, on the one hand, a word for what is all-embracing and enables us to see the whole of being as a great interconnected unity and, on the other hand, a term for individual things and events insofar as these belong to and have an effect on the whole. The degree of their reality is determined by the measure of their reality as a whole and the extent to which they concern us. The highest degree of reality is found at the level at which there is a complete unity of all the reality that can be experienced by us.

If we apply this definition of reality to the Bible, we are bound to point out in the first place that the biblical understanding of reality did not remain the same throughout the thousand years during which the different Scriptures emerged. On the contrary, it passed through a number of changes. God, the world, man and the meaning of sin—all these were understood in quite a

8

different way, for example, in the tenth century BC, at the time
of David and Solomon, from the way in which they were conceived in the sixth century BC, during the period of the Babylonian exile, or in the third century BC, when the Book of
Daniel was written. Exactly the same can, of course, be said
about the New Testament understanding of reality in the sense
in which I have defined it above. This understanding differs
considerably according to the author and the time of composition. An example of this is the emphasis which Paul gave in his
writings to the approaching end of the world—an element which
plays hardly any part at all in the later Johannine or Lucan
texts. Another Old Testament example is the different understanding in Israel of the reality of heaven and earth in the tenth
and the sixth centuries BC. In the earlier period, man was
thought of as closely bound to the earth, whereas God was seen
as reigning in heaven and surrounded by a celestial court. In the
later period, however, heaven is stripped of courtiers and only
God is there in exalted other-worldliness. Man is also no longer
bound to the earth. These examples can be multiplied and it is
important to keep these differences in the understanding of
reality that occur in the various writings of the Bible firmly in
mind if any answer is to be found to the question of the 'one'
biblical understanding of reality. It should not simply be
accepted as a matter of course that there is any one single
understanding of reality in the Bible running through all the
differences. On the other hand, however, these differences that
occur between various periods of composition of the biblical
texts should not be seen as simply negative or as something
which acts as an obstacle to their credibility. On the contrary,
they form part of the great richness of the biblical testimony.
There is a unity, but it cannot be found in a one-dimensional,
logical agreement between all the scriptural statements, but
rather in the continuity of the history of God and his dealings
with man in the Bible. This continuous history undergoes many
changes, but there is an indisputable continuity as it runs from
the earliest beginnings of Israel in the Old Testament to the
event of Christ in the New Testament. It even continues beyond
this to the present time, for the proclamation of God's activity

in Jesus Christ and the Christian mission have led to the people of the Western world and then people all over the world becoming intimately involved in this same history of God which began three thousand years ago with the people of Israel. Despite the many and often irreconcilable changes and contradictions in the biblical understanding of God, man and the world, there is nonetheless a continuous unity. The biblical writings express an increasing consciousness of God's historical activity. Indeed, if it is at all possible, despite all the tensions and contrasts that are undoubtedly present within Scripture, to compress this biblical understanding of reality into a single word, that word would certainly be 'history'.

If we speak nowadays of history, we are expressing the fact, whether we know it or not, that we are living on the spiritual legacy of the biblical tradition. It is only from the God of the Bible that the reality in which we live has been disclosed as history, as an event which is always new and open to the future, which points in the direction of unforeseeable possibilities and which can only be understood in the light of the ultimate future or the end of time. This understanding of the total reality was an expression of Israel's idea of God—Yahweh was for the people of Israel the ultimate reality and it was only in the light of the reality of Yahweh that everything else—man and the world—was comprehensible to the Israelites. For the Greek philosophers, God was the hidden background to all things who manifested himself in the inviolable order of the world. For Israel, on the other hand, God was the creator of the world who was always able to produce something new and to intervene unexpectedly in the course of his creation: 'Behold, I am the Lord, the God of all flesh; is anything too hard for me?' (Jer 32.27). This creative freedom of God can only be seen in its fulness in the light of the resurrection of Jesus and of the dead. In Rom 4.17, for instance, Paul mentions creation and the resurrection of the dead together, the God of the Bible being the one 'who gives life to the dead and calls into existence the things that do not exist'.

The living God of the Bible, then, can be distinguished from the idea of God that is found in Greek philosophy by the fact that he is seen to be free to act powerfully in the world. The Greek philosophers traced what they found to be always present and capable of experience in the world back to the presumed origin of that experience, and called it God. They did not, in this process, completely overlook the reality of God, but rather seized hold of only one aspect of that reality. The God of the Bible was moreover not only the origin of everything that is present in the world, but also, in his total freedom, the source of everything that is new and unforeseen. Very intimately connected with this is the personal character of the God of the Bible—this again in contrast to the God of the Greek philosophers. Whereas the latter is above all the remote and objective background of everything that is present, the omnipotent and free God of the Bible is a reality, encountering man in the surprising and constantly new events that he brings about.

It is in the light of this understanding of God that we can come to some conclusion regarding our understanding of all reality as history. On the one hand, in the biblical tradition, the constantly new and often astonishing events that occur in history are experienced as fundamental to that reality. (This is in striking contrast to the way in which these events were understood by the Greek philosophers and indeed by most thinkers in the ancient world, who regarded them as meaningless and chaotic). On the other hand, however, the individual events are not seen in the Bible simply in juxtaposition, temporal succession or a state of disconnected confusion. On the contrary, the God of the Bible is shown to act in each new event in the light of what he has done before in history and in most cases the earlier happening is in turn seen in a fresh light, the light thrown on it by the later event. In this way, there is in the Bible an underlying historical continuity within the series of new and extraordinary events.

This continuity should not, however, be thought of as a process of evolution in which certain tendencies from the past have an effect in the present and on the future. On the contrary, it can best be seen as a kind of bridge leading, not from the past to the present or the future, but rather in the opposite direction, that is from the historical present at any given time back into the past. This is because the biblical experience of the present, which is new at each stage in history, throws a light back on to the past, thus making man again and again mindful of the past and obliged to reconsider it in the new light of his present experience and make it his own. This historical continuity has clearly to be re-assimilated by every generation and indeed by every individual, and reconstructed so that it becomes a traditional inheritance. This is only possible when the events of history are not seen as disconnected and each new event is not regarded as having no link with all that has gone before. It is, in other words, possible for man in the Bible to see the connexion between historical events because the God who is active in each new event is the same God who was also active in the past. Because God is the same in the present and the past, each new event can, in the biblical tradition, throw a new light on the events brought about by God in the past.

This phenomenon of the continuous connexion between the new events of the present and the events of the past is known in the Bible as the faithfulness of God. God is faithful and because of this he always and unfailingly holds firm—however new and unforeseeable his present activity may be—to his earlier principles. He holds firm to man as his creation and to Israel as his people. The faithfulness of God forms the basis in the Bible of the continuity of history. Even the laws of nature do not exist in their own right—they too are free ordinances of God (see Gen 3.21 ff) and can only continue because he is free and faithful.

This historical continuity can also be seen to apply in the Bible to the way in which God fulfils his promises. These promises point explicitly to new divine activity that will take place in the life of men in the future. God, however, continues to be absolutely free even with regard to his promises, which are very rarely fulfilled in the precise literal sense in which they were understood when they were first proclaimed. Despite this, the Israelites always regarded historical events as the fulfilment of God's earlier promises because they respected God's freedom to fulfil his promises in whatever way he liked.

As an example of this we may take the promise of land, which was made to the patriarchs, and the promise of 'rest' or peace from their enemies which was closely connected with it. This promise was fulfilled when Israel had settled in the land of Palestine (Jos 21.43–45), but, as Gerhard von Rad has pointed out, 'a disturbing inconsistency remained in the fact that Israel was obliged to share this land with the Canaanites (Jg 2.3, 21, 23). This rest bestowed by God is mentioned frequently in the Bible, but it is applied to temporary conditions and is not seen in the light of ultimate fulfilment, with the result that it continued to be regarded as an open promise and the author of the letter to the Hebrews was able to interpret it in a completely new sense (Heb 3.7 ff). It is the old promise, but, in the light of the event of Christ, it discloses entirely new aspects' (G. von Rad, *Theologie des Alten Testaments*, *II*, Göttingen, 1960, p. 387; Eng. trans.: *Old Testament Theology II*, London & Edinburgh, 1965). In this way, it can be seen that the historical events which the Israelites regarded as acts brought about by their God continued to be contingent with the promises made in his name. On the one hand, this introduced an aspect of unexpectedness into the promises and, on the other, the fulfilment was given a purely provisional character. The promise pointed beyond itself to further fulfilments, with the result that the first fulfilment itself became a promise. The event of Christ and above all the raising of Jesus from the dead can be seen as fulfilling the promise of the old covenant and, going even further, it in turn becomes the promise of our participation in the life that appeared in Jesus' resurrection. This connexion between the promise and its fulfilment also acted as a norm for the development of Israel's historical consciousness and indeed for the growth of man's historical consciousness in general. The Israelites experienced within the framework of promise and fulfilment and explicitly acknowledged that there was a close link between the different but contingent events of history and that this link existed because of the faithfulness of God whose activities were contingent. It was in this way that the theme of promise and fulfilment became the basic pattern in Israel's idea of history.

Israel's writing of history is characterized by a gradual widening of the horizon of the nation's historical consciousness and a steady increase in the scope of the idea of promise and fulfilment. The first time that this conception of history is expressed in the Bible is in the tenth century account of the succession of the throne of David (2 Sam 7; 1 Kg 2). We have here a series of events that is severely restricted from the point of view of time. At the beginning of these events is the promise made to King David by the prophet Nathan that David's successors would sit on the throne in Jerusalem 'for ever' (2 Sam 7). The story then goes on to narrate the way in which this promise is fulfilled. The whole account is dominated by the question: 'Who will be the successor?' and it reports so many rivalries, intrigues and conflicts that one has the impression that the promise can never be fulfilled. The confusion ends and fulfilment is reached only when Solomon is crowned king.

The same theme of promise and fulfilment is also expressed within a much greater framework in the historiography of the Yahwist, which was written at a slightly later period. After an introductory passage outlining the earliest historical events, the author embarks on the story of the promise made to Abraham (Gen 12) and concludes his elaboration of the theme with the fulfilment of this promise in the occupation and settlement of Canaan by the people of Israel. The basic theme of promise and fulfilment is resumed in a rather different form several centuries later, in the sixth century BC, after the collapse of the state of Judah in the struggle against Babylonia, when the Deuteronomist wrote his history (found above all in the books of Kings).

The course of Israel's history is dominated by the promise in the story of the succession to the throne of David and in the Yahwistic narrative. This is vividly revealed, for example, in the descriptions of the errors committed by the persons against whom the promise had to be carried out. Even when it is proclaimed prophetically, it is clear that the promise is valid only on condition that the Mosaic law is fulfilled. It is because the law was not fulfilled that the prophets, carrying out Yahweh's commands, threatened the people of Israel with disaster long before the catastrophe in fact occurred. The editor of the Deuteronomistic account makes it quite clear, in his emphasis on the fact that the fulfilment of the promise is subject to the observance of the law, that the history of Israel ended in disaster as the result of the people's increasing guilt. The consequence of this was, of course, that the people had to leave the land that Yahweh had promised them and lose their monarchy. With the law, then, sin also became, alongside the promise, a force which determined the history of Israel.

We may therefore conclude that there is a visible tendency in all of Israel's history writing to cover an increasingly broad chronological canvas. The clear aim of this tendency was to provide a survey including every known individual event, but presented as a single great historical movement, encompassing not only the past, looking back to the creation of the world, but also the future, with its emphasis on the end of the world. The final step towards producing this great universal review of history was first made in the book of Daniel in the third century BC. This marked the beginning of the Jewish apocalyptic writing, in which what had been accomplished individually by the prophets was now systematically carried out—a presentation not only of the history of Israel, but also of the history of the whole world. The arch of this universal history spanned the whole of time, from the beginning—man's election at, or even before, his creation and that of the world—to the fulfilment which had not yet been reached—the last judgment, the coming of the Kingdom of God and the resurrection of the dead. Here, then, in the Jewish apocalyptic vision, we see for the first time the totality of reality contained within the framework of an understanding of universal history. This framework even includes the world of nature, although it is obvious that, without man, this cannot be described as history by the apocalyptic writers. In a word, then, it is clear that, in the apocalyptic vision, the whole of reality is seen as a single unity and regarded as history.

This understanding of reality, seen in the light of the biblical idea of God, is also the same as that of the early Church. The contingency of God's sovereign freedom expressed in action and his love, which, in the early Christian writings, is clearly seen to embrace the non-Jewish world as well, are, of course, far more obviously recognizable in the event of Christ than in

Judaism, where both are to some extent displaced by the emphasis on the law.

Going further, it is not difficult to trace the development of the influence of this apocalyptic and early Christian idea of history from Old and New Testament times to the Christian historical theology, for example, of Augustine in the fourth and fifth centuries, or of many of the theologians in the Middle Ages, down to the modern philosophy of history of an author such as Karl Löwith (*Weltgeschichte und Heilsgeschichte*, 1953). The modern view of history, however, is also clearly characterized by a movement away from its earlier biblical and Christian origins, resulting in man having replaced God as the subject of history and the one who acts in history. Even despite this change in emphasis that has taken place in the modern conception of history, the biblical understanding of reality has been preserved. God's providence as the force leading the course of history towards its ultimate end has been superseded, it is true, by the idea of secular progress brought about by man himself, but man's gaze is still firmly fixed on the future in a way that would hardly be possible if it were not for the deeply rooted biblical tradition of the West. The modern authors responsible for developing our present philosophy of history have, moreover, shown quite clearly that it is not possible to secularize our understanding of reality as history; if every link with the God of the Bible were rejected, that understanding would certainly be lost. The unity of history can be based, not in man, but only in God. If man is elevated to the level of the principal agent of history, as he has been since the time of the Enlightenment, the unity of history inevitably breaks up first into a multiplicity of cultures and then into a number of individual historical perspectives which is as great as the number of people who reflect in any way about the phenomenon of history itself. Again, if the unity of history is lost, the inevitable result is that the special character of history, in contrast to other conceptions of reality, is also lost. We may therefore conclude that our understanding of reality as history has not only developed from the biblical idea of God, but has also remained tied to the biblical faith in God of which it is the expression. Our understanding of all reality—including nature—as history and as a constantly new event, the meaning of which can only be decided in the future, can in the long run only continue to exist within the framework of the biblical idea of God.

Having said this, I should like to conclude this essay by comparing the biblical understanding of reality as history with two other ways of understanding reality: the cultic and mythical understanding that prevailed in many ancient cultures, and the Greek understanding of reality as cosmos.

In cultic and mythical thought, the present is meaningful only insofar as it reflects something of the symbolic events which are believed to have taken place in the very early history of the gods. The myth narrates symbolically such an event of extreme antiquity and the cult represents it in such a way as to make it acceptable to man and to sanctify his present life. For the man who thinks and lives cultically and mythically, then, the decisive event has already taken place in the early mythical period and all his endeavours are directed towards gaining a share, in his present life, in that very early event. He achieves this in the cultic process and in this way his life is clearly turned away from the future. The mythical past is the only meaningful reality for him and the future is meaningless insofar as it is unable, through cult, to play a part in the mythical past.

Even in Greek cosmic thinking, the future was also without reality. The Greeks, however, did not find reality, as those who thought cultically and mythically did, in a mythical period in the distant past. They found it rather in the eternal present, in the cosmic order of all things which could be experienced at all times. A reflection of this Greek understanding of reality is discernible in the first classic conception of natural science that emerged in the modern era: man felt himself to be living in a world of eternal and unbreakable laws which governed his own life as well as the realm of nature. For the Greeks, this idea of a cosmos or fixed order in the universe, within which every event took place according to immutable laws, was far more influential than it was during the initial period of research into physics before the emergence of modern physics at the beginning of the present century. Because the Greeks found reality not in what

was changing and fortuitous, but in cosmic order and the principle that was known in the writings of Heraclitus and the
Stoics as the *logos*, it was important for Greek man to resemble
the unchangeable *logos* as closely as possible. The Greeks therefore believed that man was governed by his own *logos* nature,
that is, by his reason, and that his salvation as an individual
and the continued existence of his soul were based on this connexion between human reason and the unchangeable *logos* that
prevailed in the cosmos. We can see, then, that those who
thought, as the Greeks did, cosmically, also lived with their
backs to the future and regarded what was new in history or
purely fortuitous as without essential reality.

It will be clear, then, how different from both the cosmic view
of the Greeks and the cultic and mythical way of thinking found
elsewhere in the ancient world the historical pattern of thought
of the Israelites was. The latter could only trust in a God who
acted with sovereign freedom. They were unable to trust, like
the Greeks, in an ordered cosmos, because that was, in their
view, simply the result of God's free ordinances. The decisive
element was not to be found in a cosmic order in the present or
in a very early happening in the past, but in the future. Both the
Israelites and the early Christians were deeply conscious that
God had, through his promises, pointed above all to the future.
According to the biblical vision, then, it is only in the light of the
future that the past and the present can be understood. Indeed,
it is only in the light of the future of the resurrection of the dead
that the past and the present will be seen as new and unexpected.

The historical view of the Bible is, however, not simply
contrasted to the understanding of reality that is found in the
cultic and mythical way of thinking on the one hand and in
Greek cosmic thought on the other. We can go further and say
that the biblical understanding of reality as history includes the
foundations of the other two views in itself. Man lives, in this
understanding of reality as history, as he does in the cultic and
mythical understanding of existence, in *traditions*. Despite our
modern tendency to strip the idea of tradition of its content,
it is still possible to observe that tradition always has a certain
affinity with mythical thought. This is discernible as a tendency
to accept what has been handed down from the past as the

reality that gives meaning to and acts as the norm for the present. In the Bible, however, this tradition has a content which is different from that found in the cultic and mythical pattern of thought. As we have seen, God's promises form the content of the biblical traditions and the events of history which are the basis of the reliability and credibility of those promises. That is why the biblical traditions point not only to a mythical event in the past, but to God's future. We have already seen that, in the biblical understanding of reality as history, the laws of nature also have a place and are regarded not simply as the ultimate reality and as absolutely unchangeable, but as the free ordinances of the faithfulness of God, who keeps the world in being through them. Man's trust has, in the biblical view, no longer to be directed towards the ordered cosmos of the natural world. Rather, man can trust in God's sovereign freedom to act in history and to determine the future. It is in God's future that this world and its laws will come to an end, that the resurrection of the dead will take place, and that there will be a new heaven and a new earth (Rev 21.1).

The biblical understanding of reality as history is therefore clearly much wider and deeper than the cosmic understanding of the Greeks or the cultic and mythical understanding of other ancient peoples. It includes the fundamental aspects of law and order on the one hand and tradition on the other. Even more important than this, however, the contingent events of history and, closely connected with this, the future itself are no longer meaningless in the biblical view, but can be seen as the free actions of God. Man no longer lives turned away from the future, but open to everything new that comes to him from the future (that is, from God). This, of course, is what is called man's openness to the world by some modern philosophers. This understanding of man is closely connected with the biblical understanding of reality as history and, like this, is a legacy of Christian thought. In the light of the God of the Bible, the reality of man and the world has been revealed to our western understanding in a hitherto unknown profundity. Finally, in this understanding of reality that originates in the Bible, we have a proof of the truth of the God of the Bible himself as the one God of all mankind.

III The Spirit of Life

1

When the second Ecumenical Council of the Church at Constantinople (381) made additions to the Nicene Creed, the Fathers' first reinforcement of the third article was a qualification of the Holy Spirit as the one who gives life. This term was of course far from novel; it recalled the New Testament descriptions of the Spirit. Paul and John in particular had spoken of the Spirit as the one who makes alive, or quickens; as the primal source of life. Nowadays that is often interpreted restrictively as a purely soteriological expression referring to the new life in faith—a topic which is undeniably at the centre of the early Christian writings. But references to the Spirit as the giver of life are certainly not to be restricted to the life of faith. There is a whole group of words which refer not only to the life-giving Spirit but explicitly to the resurrection of the dead. Paul at least is making an illusion to the breath of life that according to Gen 2.7 was breathed by God into the first man, when he says in I Cor 15.45 that whereas the first man was created a living soul the last man will be life-giving spirit. The statement that Adam was created a living soul is a direct citation of Gen 2.7. The fact that man is a living being is presented there as a result of the breath of life breathed by God into man's nostrils. This breath of life (πνοὴ ζωῆς) was conceived by Philo of Alexandria as the spirit of life (πνεῦμα ζωῆς); similarly, Paul's statement that the second Adam will be not only a living soul but life-giving spirit refers to the breath of life with which the human body was inspired by God when he made man. Hence, in order to understand the Pauline notion of the new man—the way in which the resurrected life is to be lived—we have first of all to understand the Old Testament background of that idea. And that background consists in the concept of the Spirit as the origin of all life.

That idea was far from extraordinary in the ancient world, which saw it as an empirical fact that life leaves the body with the last breath. Therefore the mysterious power of life was widely thought of as identical with breath. Hence the soul as the principle of life, and breath and spirit, went together, not only in the ancient Middle East but in Greek thought. *Pneuma* and *pnoe*, spirit and breath, were seen as closely related, and thus the word *pneuma* denotes nothing else but the air we breathe. That makes it clear how Anaximenes of Miletus, one of the earliest Greek philosophers, came to conceive the air as the origin of all things. On the same line Anaxagoras later defined the reasoning mind as the ruler of the cosmos; the main difference was that Anaximenes had thought of the human soul as an instance of the all-pervasive air, whereas Anaxagoras on the contrary conceived the power pervading the cosmos by analogy with the highest power of the human soul.

The relation between breath and air gives a better understanding of the fact that in the Old Testament the divine Spirit was seen as closely associated with wind and storm. Accordingly the biblical account of creation describes the world as originating in God's Spirit stirring the waters of the primal ocean. In a great vision the prophet Ezekiel saw the divine Spirit passing over the dead bones of his people scattered on the plain, and then when those dry bones had taken on flesh again, breathing life into them and quickening them once again in analogy to the creation of the first man.

But the most moving description of the creative effect of the divine Spirit as the origin of life is in psalm 104. The psalmist talks to God about his creatures:

> When thou hidest thy face, they are dismayed;
> when thou takest away their breath, they die
> and return to their dust.
> When thou sendest forth thy Spirit, they are created;
> and thou renewest the face of the ground.

The last phrase would seem to associate the divine Spirit with those fruitful winds which renew the vegetation in spring. Yahweh's Spirit had in fact taken over this function from Baal, who appeared in storms and bestowed fertility.

The life-giving activity of the divine Spirit is the horizon for all other functions which the Old Testament attributes to the Spirit of God. That is true especially of charismatic phenomena. Not only prophetic vision and inspiration but the work of the artist, the poet's language and the hero's deeds require a special bestowal of the Spirit of God. These charismatic effects are not however to be seen in isolation, but have to do with the same Power which inspires and animates all life. The charismatic effects are only quite outstanding instances of fulness of life. Because they display especially intensified forms of life, they must partake to an extraordinary degree of the divine Spirit.

In a similar way Paul's notion of the new life of the resurrection depends on the traditional understanding of life as the product of the divine power of the Spirit. Ordinary life is not yet life in the full sense of the word, because it is transitory. Living beings in the world as it is share only to a limited extent in the power of life, because (according to Gen 6.3) God has decided that his Spirit should not be wholly effective in men; for man is only flesh, and for that reason the time of his life is limited. When he dies, 'the dust returns to the earth as it was and the spirit returns to God who gave it', as Ecclesiastes says (9.7). That does not of course suggest any immortality of the human soul, but instead its dissolution into the divine Spirit from which it came. Paul found a reference to the limited nature of earthly life in the Genesis account of the creation of man, since it tells only of a living being or soul originating in the creative breath of life. For Paul, that meant that the living being brought forth thus was distinct from the creative Spirit and this fact explained the transient nature of our present life. Because our life in the form of a soul or as a living being is separated from its origin in the creative Spirit of God, it is subject to death. Hence the question of another life can arise, of a true life that is still connected with its origin in the Spirit. That is expressed in the Pauline idea of the resurrected life which will be one with the life-giving Spirit and therefore immortal. That notion in its turn was by no means wholly alien to the main line of Jewish tradition. The prophets, after all, had foretold an age in which the Spirit of God would rest on his people and would even be poured out on all flesh. These images refer to nothing less than eternal life, and therefore it was possible to conceive the resurrection of Christ and the spreading of the word of this event as the initial fulfilment of these ancient promises. In the New Testament the Spirit is closely associated with the risen Lord and the presence of the Spirit in the Christian community is not to be seen in isolation, separated as it were from the ongoing proclamation of Christ's resurrection in the community and from sharing through faith and hope in the saving event which is proclaimed. Although the New Testament writings when they speak of the Spirit are primarily concerned, therefore, with his charismatic presence and the new life of faith mediated by him, the profound scope of these statements and their peculiar logic are only apparent if one is aware that they are rooted in basic convictions of Jewish tradition about the Spirit as the creative origin of all life.

2

Both in the Greek Fathers and in the continuing tradition of the Orthodox East we find a continuous awareness of the fundamental meaning of the participation of the Spirit in the act of creation. It is seen as the basis of the implications of his salvific presence in the Church and in Christian experience. Of course the Greek Fathers also intellectualized their concept of the Spirit and identified the Spirit with divine wisdom. Irenaeus defended his notion that the Spirit was already present and active in the creation by reference to Proverbs 3.19: 'The Lord by wisdom founded the earth, by understanding he established the heavens, by his spirit the deeps broke forth and the clouds drop down the dew'. He also referred to the wisdom myth in the eighth chapter of the Book of Proverbs, and concluded that the one God had created and ordered everything through his word and wisdom. But in spite of the intellectualized approach of the wisdom tradition, Irenaeus related the Spirit especially to the prophetic experiences of divine inspiration. He saw those experiences not as exceptional but as exemplary of the more general fact that the Spirit of God tried 'from the very beginning' to bring all men to understand the ways of God by predicting what was to come, by telling of what had already passed, and by interpreting the present. According to Irenaeus, the Spirit was in this sense the first to have revealed God to mankind. Subsequently the Son had adopted us as children of God, and in the future of the eschaton we shall know God as the Father in his heavenly kingdom.

Although since the third century the soteriological function of the Spirit as the special divine helper in the moral destiny of man received more emphasis, especially in connexion with the rise of monasticism, Athanasius and later Basil of Caesarea stressed the operation of the Spirit in creation, in order to ensure his full divinity. In the Western Church this viewpoint was never treated quite so seriously. The action of the Spirit was seen more in connexion with love and grace than with the creation of life, and the age of the Spirit in salvation history was no longer seen as the time of mankind's preparation for the coming of the Son of God, but as the time of Church after the Incarnation and Pentecost. It is not astonishing therefore that Prenter and other commentators have spoken in reference to the Reformers of a rediscovery of the doctrine of the Spirit. To be sure, the Spirit has never been wholly forgotten in Christian theology. But in medieval theology, even in the doctrine of grace, the Spirit took a secondary place in comparison with the notion of created grace, which was taken as the supernatural gift of salvation mediated through the sacraments. The Reformers' biblicism enabled them to rediscover and apply theologically the comprehensive idea of the Spirit found in the Scriptures. To that extent both Luther and Calvin stressed the function of the Spirit in creation, although neither of them drew the systematic conclusions in regard to nature. This lack helps to explain why Protestant theology of the post-Reformation period was again restricted to a largely soteriological conception of the action of the Spirit.

That is especially true of Pietism. At the beginning of the seventeenth century, Johann Arndt said nothing about the co-operation of the Spirit in the work of creation. Later Jean de Labadie expressly rejected the idea, and although Philipp Jakob Spener mentioned the doctrine, he treated it as a fragment of a dead tradition. Hence the Spirit of God was increasingly treated as a matter of Christian piety; as a subjective experience, and never as a principle of the theological understanding of nature. The Cartesian dualism of spirit and matter certainly made its contribution to the generally lastingly effective influence of this subjective understanding of the doctrine of the Spirit.

The subjectivist trend in the notion of the Spirit was further strengthened by the influence of the spiritualistic movements of sixteenth and seventeenth centuries which originated in medieval mysticism. In this tradition, which also influenced Pietism, the Spirit was related to the study of man but not to the natural world. The Spirit was associated with the teaching of the inner light in the human consciousness. That prepared the way for the identification of spirit and consciousness in the idealist tradition, as became the rule in the aftermath of Cartesian dualism. Even John Locke conceived the Spirit as the substance which is the active principle in the operations of the mind, and because David Hume eliminated the notion of substance, he was able to do away with the idea of the Spirit altogether. The idealistic philosophers on the other hand, and Hegel especially, developed a new conception of the universe as the creation of the Spirit. But they did so on the basis of Cartesian dualism and an identification of Spirit and consciousness. It was precisely this point that proved so fateful for idealism, since Hegel's notion of Spirit as absolute consciousness could be shown to be a projection of the human consciousness into the dimension of the absolute. Hence the identification of spirit and consciousness became a major argument for the atheism of Feuerbach and his famous successors. But Christian theology too had to reject the idealist notion of spirit, precisely because of the identification of the divine with the human spirit. The theological critique of idealism led to a separation of the divine Spirit from human consciousness. But, simultaneously, theological discourse about the divine

Spirit lost its empirical connexion, and thus became almost wholly meaningless. The sole function still attributed to talk about the Spirit is that of a pretended legitimation for otherwise unintelligible assertions of faith. Such a conception of the work of the Spirit is of course far from banishing the subjectivism that has become so characteristic of Christian piety in the modern era. Such recourse to the Spirit represents on the contrary the apex of that subjectivism—the subjectivism, in other words, of an irrational act of faith.

It should be obvious that recourse to a supra-rational principle which makes acceptable what is otherwise inconceivable, is not (as far as theologians are concerned) an acceptable basis for a responsible doctrine of the Holy Spirit. But such a doctrine cannot be worked out on a basis of the identification of Spirit and mind, not at least since that identification has met with such serious and effective criticism in the history of post-Hegelian thought. But it is not advisable to attempt any new establishment of the notion of the Spirit in the context of a phenomenology of religious experience, especially the experience of 'spiritual' rebirth, for such pretended empirical realism would in fact lead back into the blind alley of subjectivist decisionism. In order to find an appropriate starting-point for a renewed doctrine of the Spirit, we have to move back behind the whole subjectivist line in the history of the doctrine, and behind an isolated concentration on the soteriological function of the Spirit. The only thing that can overcome the subjectivist restriction of traditional Christian piety and Christian thought in regard to the Spirit is a new understanding of the Spirit in relation to the biblical statements about his role in creation, and in regard to the possible contribution of a doctrine of the Spirit to a theology of nature. But we have to ask if there is any intellectually responsible way of relating the Holy Spirit to the interpretation of nature.

3

In modern Christian thought there have been two outstanding attempts to escape from the subjectivist impasse in under-

standing the Spirit. In both cases the intention was to work out a
new idea of the Spirit within the broad framework of a theology
of life. One of these projects is the chapter on life and spirit in
the third volume of Tillich's *Systematic Theology*. The other is
Teilhard de Chardin's vision of an evolutionary life process
directed from a spiritual centre.

Tillich sees spirit as one of the 'dimensions of life' alongside
the inorganic, organic and mental (or psychological). All these
dimensions are present potentially in every living being. Among
them spirit is the 'power of animation' and thus distinct from the
various parts of the organic system. For Tillich spirit is not
identical with consciousness, though on the level of human life
the self-consciousness of the creature is included in the socio-
personal dimension, which Tillich calls spirit. Hence man is that
creature in whom the dimension of spirit has become dominant.
On the other hand, even the human spirit is unable to master
life's ambiguities in its basic functions of self-integration, self-
creation and self-transcendence. The human spirit can overcome those ambiguities only with the help of God's Spirit.
Therefore Tillich distinguishes divine Spirit from human spirit.
Only by special ecstatic activity can the human spirit share in
divine Spirit; and only in that way (Tillich asserts) can the
human spirit attain to the integration and unity of the three
areas of spiritual life: culture, morality and religion.

Tillich was conscious of a far-reaching similarity between his
own conception of the relation between spirit and life and
Teilhard de Chardin's ideas. He read *The Phenomenon of Man* only
when his own book was complete. In fact the two thinkers
approach one another in the fundamental notion that the spirit
is the animating power of all life and as such is not identical with
the conscious mind, even though it is manifest in a decisively
new and intensified form in the emergence of human consciousness. Teilhard and Tillich are also alike in their emphasis on
the self-transcendence of life, which Teilhard thinks of as
'radial energy', whereas for Tillich it is the same phenomenon
which relates human spirit to divine Spirit.

There are however differences between the two conceptions.
First, Teilhard does not make the same distinction as Tillich

between divine Spirit and spirit as a dimension of life. In Teilhard's view there is only one spirit which permeates and activates all material processes and drives them beyond themselves to progressive spiritualization and convergent union towards a centre of perfect unity which, though the end of the evolutionary process, is also the true source of its dynamic power. In that perspective the created spirit can be seen only as participation in the dynamics of the one spirit which animates the whole process of evolution. What is more, in such a perspective the difference between God and creature is maintained since material beings participate in the spiritual dynamics only by self-transcendence. This corresponds to Tillich's stress on the self-transcendence of life and the ecstatic element in spiritual experience. Tillich probably retained the dualism of spirit and divine Spirit for the sake of his method of correlating question and answer. Nevertheless, even in his conceptual framework, it is difficult to understand why he keeps the ecstatic element of a 'spiritual presence' of God in faith, hope and love, instead of seeing it as a general characteristic of spiritual experience in the self-transcendence of life.

A second difference between Tillich and Teilhard is that Teilhard does not use the vague and confusing image of 'dimensions of life' which has at best a certain metaphorical value when it shows the 'one-dimensional' inadequacy of a purely materialistic description of organic life. The weakness of this metaphor and the resulting confusion arise from the fact that there is of course no co-ordinate system of 'dimensions' of the inorganic, organic, mental and spiritual. The same interest in the depth and complexity of the phenomenon of life eludes a purely materialistic description, but was expressed much more simply by Teilhard de Chardin in terms of a spiritual interior of every material phenomenon. He shared that idea with the ancient tradition of animism. But he also tried to justify it: first by the principle that scientific investigation should always look for a general rule behind so apparently extraordinary a phenomenon as the emergence of human consciousness; and second by his thesis of a regular correspondence between the degree of complexity of a material phenomenon and the extent of its spiritual inwardness. Teilhard's most daring notion was however his combination of the spiritual interior of natural phenomena with the energy determining natural processes.

Ultimately (according to Teilhard) all energy is spiritual. Since however energy becomes accessible to physical observation in the relations between physical phenomena, Teilhard put forward his famous distinction between a tangential energy or force which explains the various forms of solidarity of bodily elements and their interactions, and a radial energy apparent in the self-transcendence of phenomena towards increasing complexity and unity. This distinction is very closely associated with the fundamental thesis of the spiritual nature of all energy. Scientists, especially physicists, are concerned (so Teilhard insisted) only with the outward manifestation of cosmic energy in corporeal interactions. But if energy, as Teilhard assumed, is essentially spiritual, then energy must have another aspect, which is in fact apparent in dynamic self-transcendence, which Teilhard called radial energy.

The problems associated with his idea are especially clear when we ask what aspects of the concept of energy are missing from Teilhard's approach. Here the phenomenon of an energy field deserves particular attention. Classical mechanics was concerned with bodies, with their positions in space and time, and with the forces which take effect in their interactions. Those forces were attributed to the bodies which were said to exert force in acting. But the attempt of physicists to reduce the notion of natural force to a characteristic of bodies, and especially to their mass, failed. Einstein was in fact the last to make such an attempt. Yet his theory of relativity led to the opposite conclusion. Instead of revealing space as a property of bodies and their interactions, the theory of relativity produced the conception of matter as a function of space. That, as C. F. von Weizsäcker has shown, was the definitive transition from a notion of natural force dependent on the model of the moving body, to an independent idea of energy as a field. Conceiving natural forces as fields of energy, as for example in the case of an electrical or a magnetic field, means seeing energy as the fundamental, autonomous reality which transcends the body through which it manifests itself. Energy conceived as a field is a reality which can be thought of autonomously and not only as an attribute of a body as its subject.

Teilhard de Chardin was unable fully to evaluate this radical transformation by which natural force as a property of bodies became an autonomous reality which is merely manifested in the origin and motion of bodies. To be sure, Teilhard recognized the concept of energy as the basic notion of physics. But he expressed reservations in regard to the Einsteinian field theory. He insisted on the association of energy with a body, and expressed that connexion in his idea of energy as a kind of spiritual interior of bodies, even inorganic bodies.

In regard to Teilhard's notion of spirit, raising the problems associated with this concept of energy may seem like side-stepping the issue. But it is clear that Teilhard's decision to see energy not in terms of field but as the inwardness of bodies, had far-reaching consequences for his idea of spirit. To a certain extent this notion of energy is diametrically opposed to his fundamental conception of spirit as a transcendent principle which exceeds all given reality, yet activates it in the direction of creative unification. If Teilhard had conceived energy as a field, that would have fully accorded with his basic idea of the Spirit whose creative power determines the whole process of evolution precisely because his reality exceeds that of all individual creatures and species. Since however Teilhard was unable to advance beyond the notion of energy as the interior of bodies, he ascribed energy to bodies so to speak as their subject. Therefore he was compelled to attribute even the movement of the self-transcendence of living creatures, and thus the entire dynamics of evolution, to the action of these finite beings, instead—as he in fact wished—of referring to a principle which transcended all finite phenomena and which he called Omega. Here we are faced with the fundamental ambiguity which permeates Teilhard's thought; the ambiguity of his explanation of the ultimate mover of the evolutionary process: point Omega *or* self-evolving beings. If energy is ascribed to bodies, then the process and direction of evolution seem to derive from self-developing forms of life and species acting as though they were the active subjects of their own evolution. In this perspective

point Omega becomes a mere extrapolation of tendencies
inherent in the evolutionary process or, more exactly, self-
developing creatures. But Teilhard on the contrary wanted to
define point Omega, the goal of evolution, as its true creative
source. He succeeded in doing so—by describing evolution as
the work of the Spirit whose reality exceeds that of all individual
entities and is ultimately identical with God Omega in his
progress towards the creative unification of his world at each
new stage of its development. Unfortunately Teilhard failed to
relate his vision of the world process as creative unification from
its divine goal with his notion of energy, although in his philosophy spirit and energy characterize the same reality. He could
think of energy only as interior to bodies, instead of seeing it as a
field, which transcends the bodies in which it appears and takes
priority over them. If Teilhard had seen the nature of energy
in terms of field, he would have made more consistent and
convincing his central intuition of the world as a process of
creative unification through a spiritual dynamics at work in it.
He would not have been forced to abandon the idea of a spiritual
inside of corporeal phenomena. He would only have had to add
that what was in question was the way in which the universal
field of cosmic energy appeared from the angle of the finite
entities through which it manifested itself. These finite things
participate in the universal field of cosmic energy only by
simultaneously transcending themselves, as if in ecstasy, and
the degree to which they are capable of such ecstatic experience is the extent of their spirituality. In this way Tillich's
insight into the ecstatic nature of spiritual presence is referred
far beyond the specific spirituality of Christian faith, love and
hope, to which it is confined in Tillich's own perspective.
Instead of characterizing a mere peculiarity of Christian experience, it indicates a basic trait of all finite reality and
especially of organic life.

4

The proposed revision of Teilhard's idea of evolution makes it
possible to refute a number of the most important arguments

against his theses. Above all it enables us to dispense with the notion of a teleological orientation of the process of evolution, and leaves much more room for an element of chance or contingency in it. But we must still ask whether it is justifiable to use the term spirit to describe the energy effective in evolution. Is there any real theological significance in that use of the word 'spirit'. And is there a substantial connexion with the way in which the Christian tradition of the Spirit of God spoke of the Spirit as the creative source of all life.

I shall examine this question by inquiring first into the conditions for an appropriate translation of the biblical idea of a creative Spirit as the origin of all life into the context of modern thought. In that case certain criteria come into play which can be applied subsequently to Teilhard's thought and to the model that arose from my discussion of it.

Any attempt to translate the ideas of an earlier epoch must first take into account the gulf which the translation has to bridge. Most of the differences between the biblical and modern understanding of life can be attributed to the fact that the biblical idea of life starts from the assumption of a source of life which is to be sought outside the creature, as was empirically evident to antiquity in the phenomenon of breath, whereas modern biology thinks of life as a function of the living, self-reproductive cell. At first this comparison reveals a sharp contrast between the modern, immanentist conception of life and the Old Testament interpretation of life from the basis of a transcendent principle.

In comparison with this fundamental opposition, the question whether that transcendent principle is to be called spirit seems secondary. On closer inspection, however, the two notions of life are seen to contradict one another in more than one respect. On the one hand, the biblical perspective leaves room for the idea of an independent existence which is the essence of a living being: it has life in itself. On the other hand, in its analysis of the phenomenon of life, modern biology does not simply exclude everything that cannot be derived from the living cell. Although life is conceived as the activity of a living cell or a higher organism, that activity itself is still conditioned, and especially by the requirement of an environment fit for the organism: a milieu which is the first precondition of its continuing to live. Once parted from such an environment, no organism can persist. In that sense every organism depends on specific conditions in order to live, and those conditions are not merely external to its living but make it possible and are characteristic of it; an organism lives 'in' its environment. It not only requires living-space, a territory which it actively possesses, but it transforms that environment into a means of self-realization; it is nurtured by its environment in the literal and metaphorical sense. In that sense every organism exists in a movement beyond itself. Again we see that life is essentially ecstatic: it takes place in an interaction of the creature and its milieu, not only within the confines of the organism in terms of itself.

Is there any connexion between that ecological self-transcendence of life and the biblical idea of the Spirit as the source of life? The answer would seem to be yes. To discern the relation, we first concentrate on what has been said about the phenomenal form of spirit, and leave aside for a moment its divine character. It is clear that for us too breath is among the most important environmental conditions of life. Only with air to breathe, can organic processes continue. In the context of the modern understanding of life, the phenomenon of breath is an appropriate illustration of the dependence of the organism on its environment. But we can no longer think of breath as the actual source of life. In this regard all modern notions of life depart from the primitive interpretation which also lies behind the corresponding biblical statements. Nevertheless there is an element of truth in that primitive idea of life, and the key is to be found in the dependence of the organism on its environment.

It would of course be too extreme to assert that a creature is a direct creation of its environment, even though appropriate environmental conditions are a prerequisite of its life and survival. But in the creature's self-transcendence in the course of its life, and in its transformation of its environment into the location and means of its life, the creature also relates to its own future or, more precisely, to the future of its own transformation. That occurs in every act of self-production, of self-nurture, of the regeneration and reproduction of one's own life. By its drives, every living creature is orientated (though not always consciously) to its individual future and to the future of its species. That too is part of the ecstatic nature of the self-transcendence of life; it is what Teilhard de Chardin called 'radial energy'. The most impressive evidence for that is the increasing complexity and ultimate convergence of the evolutionary life-process, but it also occurs in the individual's life and especially in the temporal aspect of his self-transcendence. If it was justifiable to revise Teilhard's notion of 'radial energy' in the sense of an energy field determining the evolutionary process, another assumption appears reasonable: namely, that this energy field is manifest in the self-transcendence of creatures, and thus produces the existence of individuals no less than their realization of life. Hence the truth in the ancient idea of breath as the creative origin of life is not cancelled by the dependence of the organism on its environment; this image in fact holds a more profound mystery closely related to the ecological self-transcendence of life: temporal self-transcendence in the life-process of every living creature is a specific phenomenon of organic life which distinguishes it from inorganic structures.

At this point a number of questions occur which demand further investigation. In the first place there is the problem of the relation between ecology and genetics. The description offered of the self-transcendence of life has been largely concerned with ecological phenomena. But does it also apply to genetic facts? If that were not so, the assumption of an energy field effective in the self-transcendence of life would seem much less convincing. A second group of questions concerns the specific nature of this 'field'. Is it justifiable to use the field concept in relation to the meaning of the future for the present, with which Teilhard's God Omega and the creative effect Teilhard claimed Omega had on the whole process of evolution are associated? In that case the field concept would replace the traditional idea of a goal-directedness, an inner teleology of natural events. Is the field concept appropriate here? In any case, the temporal structure of field theories would have to be

studied more thoroughly, especially in the light of problems of
quantum theory, which no longer abstracts from time, as other
field theories do. This raises an associated question: what is the
rôle of the contingency of natural events in the effectiveness
of such a field? Finally, even if we are sure that we can conceive
the creative efficacy of Teilhard's point Omega in terms of an
energy field, we still have to show the relevance of that possibility to the phenomenon of spirit.

5

Teilhard's and Tillich's theories of spirit and life allowed us the
suggestion that the self-transcendence of life should be used as a
key to the phenomenon of spirit and as a starting-point for a
re-interpretation of spiritual reality. This proposal arose in part
from Tillich's idea of the ecstatic nature of spiritual experience,
but does not accord with Tillich in the separation of that
ecstatic experience from the general phenomenon of the life
process, because the latter ultimately derives its vitality from
its self-transcendence. Tillich's separation of the presence of the
Spirit in the theological sense from ongoing self-transcendence in
the life of all living things is comprehensible on the supposition
(not controverted by Tillich) that the self-transcendence of life is
merely a matter of the creature's own activity. Teilhard's
theory of spirit and energy, and the replacement of Teilhard's
notion of 'radial energy' by that of an energy field effective in the
process of evolution, allows us to see the self-transcendence of the
life process in a more complex way. The self-transcendence of
life is conceived both as an activity of the creature and as the
effect of a power which takes the living being above its limits and
preserves that being through its life. The functions of the self-
creation and self-integration of life are dependent on that
ongoing self-transcendence. If the self-transcendence of life
could be exhaustively explained as an autonomous activity of
the living creature, there would be no room for the assumption of
a spiritual reality as the source of its life. But if the complex
phenomenon of self-transcendent life demands a dual defini-

tion, it seems reasonable to speak of the Spirit as the source of life.

Jn this more comprehensive application to the phenomenon of life as a whole, as suggested by biblical usage, the notion of Spirit also indicates that the self-transcendent activity of organic life is to be understood in the broader context of the evolutionary process, insofar as that process is orientated to a definitive self-affirmation of life, but is also characterized by a profusion of fragmentary forms of the power and beauty of life, in which the creative and unifying activity of life also anticipates the ultimate goal of its evolutionary process.

The re-definition of the concept of spirit on the basis of the self-transcendence of all organic life cancels the restriction of spirit to human consciousness. Spirit is neither identical with consciousness nor manifested primarily in consciousness. Nevertheless man's reflective mind represents a specific form and a new stage of participation in the power of Spirit, and that is the special mode of human self-transcendence.

Man does not transcend himself only in his environment and from its resources. He does not only transform his milieu by appropriating it as his own. He is also capable of methodically changing his world, in order to alter the conditions of his own existence. That presupposes first that man is able to conceive the phenomena of his world as they actually are and not only in relation to his drive-governed wishes. Man can 'empathize' materially with things distinct from himself in a way open to no other creature. The second presupposition of the methodical transformation of the world by human activity is that man is capable of projecting a future different from his present. That makes him master of his present. Both aspects depend on the even more basic presupposition that man can take up a position beyond himself and so to speak study himself from that vantage-point. In other words, he has the ability to reflect. The reflective human consciousness emphatically illustrates the specifically human form of existence beyond oneself. Precisely because he is beyond himself, man is himself. Not only that specific individual, but as such a man generically: a human being. Because however it must take up a standpoint beyond itself, the human

consciousness cannot of itself guarantee the unity of its experience, but is orientated to a reality beyond itself which guarantees
the unity of its experiences. We conceive the particular only
within a wider horizon of significance which is always anticipated as a unified reality. That underlies all abstract thought.
But the unity which grounds the individual life beyond itself is
also experienced as concrete in human community. In the
uniquely reflective human consciousness the meaning of
society for the individual has a new characteristic: society in its
difference from the individual becomes constitutive for the
individual's experience of the unity and identity of his own
existence. In this particular way man is a social being, not
merely as the member of a mass, but by recognizing society, for a
community of human life is expressed in society which is
superior to its individual members inasmuch as that community
grounds the very humanity of the individual. Insofar as society
consists only of individuals, the ultimate basis of its unity must
lie beyond the concrete institutions of society: as a social being
man is also a religious being.

It is obvious that the specific form of human self-transcendence characterizes all those human activities and achievements
which are spiritual (that is, intellectual or cultural) in a narrow-
er sense. The self-transcendence of human world-openness and
eccentricity is expressed in the human capacity for abstract
thought as well as in trust, love and hope. It is just as fundamental to the individual's quest for his individual identity as to
social life and its institutions, and not last to the creation of a
cultural world on the basis of a symbolic world of meaning and
language. In all these achievements man is both creatively free
and a creation of the spiritual reality which raises him above
and beyond himself. The most decisively creative acts of his
spiritual life are the most impressive evidence for this: the
creative design of an artist, the sudden discovery of a truth, the
experience of liberation in a moment of significant existence, the
power of a moral commitment; all that takes hold of us by some
kind of inspiration. All such experiences bear witness to the
reality of a power which raises up our hearts—the power of the
Spirit. When man is most creative, he is most conscious of being

grasped by a spiritual power which raises him above himself. Its presence characterizes not only rare moments of spiritual elevation, but permeates our life even on the level of everyday behaviour, which is profoundly open to the world even in the negative movement of reserve. The extraordinary experiences of spiritual freedom and creativity are not exceptional but are uniquely characteristic of human existence in general.

Nevertheless human life is not fully joined to the power of the Spirit. We all know depression and discontent. We all know moments in which our life seems without any real unity and meaning. Conflicts, oppression and violence occur among individuals and in relations between individual and social world. There are failure and guilt, disability, sickness and death. But there are also moments in which a meaningful and happy life shines forth, if only fragmentarily; and in the moment of death our life as a whole is still an open question. There is certainly room enough for the play of life's ambiguities which Tillich portrayed so aptly. For that reason experiences of tenderness or mutual trust—experiences which give our life hope and significance—feel supernatural, especially when they offer our life a lasting identity and integrity, in spite of all its fragility and uncertainty. The Christian message with its assurance of a new life that will no longer be subject to death, provides a new and unshakable confidence, a new presence of the Spirit. Its living centre is the prospect of being related to God's future; a prospect embodied in the person of Christ and ever since effective in human history. But the Spirit of this new life, lived in the community of the faith, is none other than that which animates and quickens all living things. Only because it is the same Spirit that by the inspiration of life's overwhelmingly rich self-transcendence is the source of all life, the Spirit active in the Christian community is no escapist opiate or piety, but that Power which enables the faithful to bear and finally vanquish the absurdities and disappointments of the world as it is.

IV Man—the image of God?

In the history of mankind hitherto, the meaning of human existence has for the most part been understood in religious terms. People were not dealing solely with tangible things, actual circumstances and processes, but were conscious of facing invisible powers, on which the success or failure of human life depended. They tried at least to get to know the character of these powers which are beyond human control, and to enter into some relation with them. For thousands of years that was the theme of religious knowledge and worship. As member of a worshipping community, man became a client and companion of the divine power which he adored. This gave his life a deeper meaning. The processes of nature and of human society, the everyday concerns of the individual, the dangers, catastrophes and culminating experiences of life, all fitted into a meaningful pattern which extended far beyond the immediately tangible and manageable, and because it did so, encompassed and supported the life of the individual, his kindred and his people.

People nowadays, however, appear largely to have lost any feeling for the powers or the power with which religions are concerned, or at least it seems to have become very faint. We consider the forces at work in nature, in human behaviour and in society as capable of being rationally investigated and mastered. Nature and society have given up their mysteries before the progress of science. Is there any place left there for divine powers? To many people nowadays it seems more obvious that men have made gods in their own image than that man is made to the image and likeness of a god.

In fact, the breath-taking advances of modern science and

technology have created the impression that man has dislodged God by hoisting himself into mastery of the world. In this connexion, strange to say, it is often overlooked that man's actual mastery over the world is part of the biblical idea of his being made to the image of God; so it obviously cannot necessarily involve human rivalry with God. Furthermore, men are far from having achieved likeness to God. It is notable that an atheist such as Jean Paul Sartre, like Nietzsche, can speak only of man's *desire* to be God. The desire betrays distance from the goal that is sought. And nowhere does a human being miss the possible present fulfilment of his life so fundamentally as when he lives his life under the domination of such a desire. If there is any possibility for men of experiencing a plenitude of life even in the present, that experience will have to come in the midst of the deficiencies of their own condition and conduct, not just after the definitive and total elimination of those inadequacies. It is part of the mystery of life that its fulfilment can be sensed, and even laid hold of as a present happiness, in and despite its fragility, even in face of failure or under the disfigurement of malice. Where that happens, it is always a gift; it can never be forced. A power is revealed there, granting or refusing, which rules in everyday life as much as in extraordinary events. To be conscious of this mysterious power, to sense its operation, is a mark of the religiously aware human being.

One often hears the view nowadays that religions and religious sentiment belong to an outgrown stage of human development. Certainly much in the traditional religions has irrecoverably gone; the same thing has happened in other departments of life. Religion and religious piety themselves, however, need no more have disappeared than medicine, for instance, which has also changed considerably since the days of Hippocrates. Those who talk of the end of religions in general, lay themselves open to the suspicion that they have lost sight of the central mystery of human life, the sudden gleam and withdrawal of fulfilment in the midst of all its fragility and limitations. The relation of the divine reality to which the religious sense is directed, to the facts of nature and history which were experienced and handed down by earlier generations as a

medium of divine presence, has changed and will continue to
change. Nevertheless, the religious sense of the power or powers
which decide the plenitude of life, does not thereby lose its
meaning. It has been a characteristic of man from the beginning,
just as much as his ability to use fire and tools. Serious philosophical prejudice is evident in the fact that present-day philosophical anthropology so often either completely overlooks this
phenomenon or treats it as quite marginal. No attempt to define
the specific features of human behaviour can disregard the
fact that man, as we know him in history, appeared on the stage
of this world as a religious being.

Man and his gods belong together. That is the element of
truth in the anthropological interpretation of religion as a
reflection of man, his longings, wishes and fears. Human beings
have always seen themselves, and their own nature, destiny and
position in the world, in the mirror of the divine power which
they adored. This in itself shows that the gods are not a superfluous double of man. Without them, man would not at all be
the being hungry for eternity and perfection which in the mirror
of his gods he knows himself to be. So it is pointless to assert that
man made his gods rich and perfect at the expense of his own
idea of himself, which is what Ludwig Feuerbach meant by his
talk of man's religious self-alienation. Friedrich Nietzsche
expressed the same view: ' . . . man has not dared to ascribe
all his strong and astonishing factors to himself . . . by conceiving
everything great and strong in man as superhuman, and foreign
to him, man belittled himself'. That is not the case, because it was
only in the light of the divine power that man discovered the
wealth of his own destiny.

Only the religious experience of the mysterious depth of the
reality which grants or refuses fulfilment to human life, raised
human beings above what lies nearest at hand, the humdrum
everyday, and opened their eyes to the vast world as a whole
and man's tasks and possibilities in it. Religious exaltation
bestowed on men the wealth of an inner life which becomes
aware of its own limitations and its own failure, and precisely
thereby lives in the presence of what is perfect. Through
religion they came to know the splendour and consolation of a life

raised above everyday cares and pleasures. They knew themselves as favoured and grace-endowed by the gods, and where the grace that only a god can grant was refused them, the life they led apart from such divine fulfilment confronted them with all its staleness and pitiful futility. Religions are always ultimately concerned with men's participation in the glory and power of the gods.

It is not surprising, then, that men so often thought of their gods as possessing those very perfections which they themselves shared in through the experience of religious exaltation. This shows the solidarity of gods and men in the life of the religions. It is the foundation of all anthropomorphic representation of the gods. Such a mode of representation by no means presupposes a primitive, uncultivated mind. The contrary is the case. It indicates a high degree of discernment and culture for men to perceive a face of a human kind in the depth of the powerful manifestations of divine powers in the life of nature and society, and therefore of the community of the gods with men. This solidarity of divine and human cannot be correctly understood if it is reduced by definition to the mere act of human beings sketching an idealized picture of themselves. Instead man always and only finds and achieves himself in this mirror. That is what is involved in calling man an image of God: his being, and the mysterious divine power which decides the success or failure of human life, belong together, but in such a way that man discovers and achieves his own being only on the basis of his experience of God; this fact lies at the root of all anthropomorphic ideas and representation of God and gods.

If we look for a translation of the idea of man as the image of God into the language of a modern doctrine of man, probably man's *personality* would best correspond to the Old Testament concept of likeness to God. That may sound surprising at first, yet it is possible to show not only common structural features, but links in the history of ideas between personality and the idea of man as the image of God. The Bible contains no verbal equivalent of the modern idea of person. The nearest objective equivalent to that *dignity* of man which is most closely linked with personality, is nevertheless found precisely in the Old Testament idea. For his quality as God's image is the basis of the inviolability of man for man, the prohibition of shedding human blood: 'Whosoever sheds the blood of man, by man shall his blood be shed; for God made man in his own image' (Gen 9.6). To attack the life of a human being is to commit an offence against God. That is certainly a specifically religious justification of the inviolability of human life. But even in our modern conviction of the inviolability of the person, the religious motive lies quite close to the surface. For, of course, it is by no means self-evident and is not entailed by any empirical findings of the science of man, that human life must be inviolable and that the personal centre of a fellow human being remains beyond the power of anyone else to determine. If we respect in our fellow man a centre of personal self-determination beyond our control, this is not as it were a fact to be ascertained by the methods of natural science, but an attitude of faith. People could perhaps be mistaken about this in former days, but at all events our century has learnt that it is perfectly possible to exceed that limit and dispose of human beings as though they were things: not only their bodies, but even their minds and emotional life. What is specifically human is, of course, crushed thereby. But unfortunately that is just as possible as it is to deal with nature and history without perceiving God's reality in them. In both cases our own behaviour sets up the barrier which prevents the experience of a human personal partner as well as that of God's reality. A fellow human being can only be experienced as a personal partner if his personal self-determination is respected as inviolable. But at the basis of such respect lies a reserve which does not derive from the relationship to this or that human being, but springs from deeper roots. This reverence for the person of one's fellow man corresponds to the reference to man as the image of God with which the Old Testament justified its prohibition of murder.

The modern idea of human personality is, of course, not purely biblical in origin. The word comes from the Latin; *persona*, like the corresponding Greek word *prosopon*, first of all means the human face or countenance, and then the mask which identified an actor's rôle; only later in legal language did it come to mean the unique individual. The word obviously lent itself particularly well to this purpose, because the face is especially expressive of the characteristics of the individual human being. The word only assumed its full content in early Christian times. In the theological controversies of the ancient Church about the three divine persons and the unity of Jesus' person in which both divine and human are united, the concept of person was more precisely thought out. The outcome indicates in a remarkable way the solidarity of divine and human, which we have already noted in the idea of man's creation in the likeness of God. In the early sixth century the Roman Boethius, minister of the Ostrogothic King Theodoric, formulated the classic definition: person is the individual substance of a rational nature. Not every individual existent is a person, therefore, but only the individual endowed with reason. The statement is strikingly reminiscent of the Greek description of man as a rational animal. Participation in reason, *logos*, distinguishes man from the brute animals and is the ground of his personality. Reason, however, in Greek thought was not simply an attribute of man, but characterized what is truly divine; and man's participation in reason, his capacity to grasp the *Logos* which prevails throughout the universe, marks his participation in the divine.

We have seen that the modern idea of human personality has a starting-point in the Old Testament and another root in Greek thought. Both roots are religious in character, and point to man's solidarity with the divine realm, to his creation in the image and likeness of God. It is no accident that early Christian theologians recognized the familiar Old Testament teaching in the Greek conception of man as a rational being. As early as the second century, the Old Testament statement that God created man to his image and likeness was interpreted in the sense that God bestowed his *logos* on man, the same *logos* which was to appear fully and completely in Jesus. And this means that only by Jesus was man's destiny, his true humanity, fully realized; in accordance with the New Testament idea that only Jesus is the perfect image of God, and from the beginning was the criterion for the divine creation of man. Only the man who is fully united with God and his immortal life brings man's nature to fulfilment. That corresponds to the fact that from the

beginning of human history men discovered themselves
indirectly through the knowledge they were able to gain about
the gods. The fact that man is not truly man without his god,
was fully confirmed by the Christian faith in the perfect union
of God with a human being through whom God has also united
himself with humanity as a whole, because by his unity with
God this one human being has manifested true human perfection, the humanity of man as such.

This brought new dynamism to the idea of man's solidarity
with God, his likeness to God. Man is not complete from the
start as an image of God. He has a history which is directed to the
attainment of his destiny, to the realization of true and perfect
humanity in union with God. The goal of this history of man's
becoming man has already appeared in Jesus, and this sets the
theme for all subsequent history: all human beings are to come
to share in the truly human character which appeared in him.
Man's being as a person is involved in this historical movement.
As a person, the individual is directed towards the as yet
incompletely achieved humanity of man. This is precisely why
respect for the personal mystery of other human beings is
required. It does not yet appear what we shall be, and everyone's
life is affected by this mystery. This is what is violated when a
human being is judged and treated solely by what achievements
and abilities he can be found to have that are useful for society.
To respect one's fellow man as a person always means not to
reduce him to what is visible about him. The eyes of love do not
see in the beloved only what everyone sees; they see him in the
light of his mystery as a person, his divine destiny.

These last statements already anticipate the specifically
Christian sense of personality. We recall that in Christian
theology the Greek idea of man as a rational being was brought
into relation with the Old Testament statement that God
created man in his own image and likeness, and to the New
Testament concept that only in Jesus was the image of God, and
therefore the true perfection of humanity, fully manifested.
The Greek idea of man as a rational being was therefore
increasingly transformed by Old Testament and specifically
Christian features. That is the way in which the modern idea of

human personality historically arose. When we speak nowadays of man as a person, we surely mean more than that he is a being endowed with reason.

This 'more' has already been referred to in what I said about personal self-determination. For present-day opinion, what makes a human being human is not primarily the fact that he grasps in a rational way the *Logos* that prevails throughout the universe. Such knowledge perhaps exceeds the scope of human capacity? So we are more inclined to be sceptical. But what does seem to present-day judgment inalienably to belong to man as a person is personal self-determination: freedom of judgment and decision.

The theme of freedom was not, of course, first raised by Christian theology, but theology anchored it in the centre of man's understanding of himself. Precisely in his freedom, man is the image of God, who creates everything from nothing. The Old Testament idea of man as the image of God already placed great emphasis on the function of the image to represent the dominion of a ruler in his domain, especially in his absence. That is how man represents the presence of God and his dominion in the world created by him. The vocation to exercise the divine dominion over the world, forms, according to the biblical account of creation, the basis of man's special position among all the creatures. That idea was developed by Christian theology in ever new ways, and was connected with human freedom. A culminating point here is comprised by the formulations of the fifteenth-century German cardinal, Nicholas of Cusa. He defined man's freedom as likeness to God in creative production, particularly in intellectual projects and technical models. This idea contains one of the presuppositions for the relation of man to the world in the modern period of history, characterized by rational construction and technology.

The idea of freedom, however, is concerned not only with man's dominion over the world, but with his relation to himself, his fellow men and society. In this wide sense, Hegel's philosophy gave a profound interpretation to freedom in the modern sense as a fruit of the Christian belief in the Incarnation. It grew, he claimed, from the union of man with absolute truth,

which at first was believed only as having occurred in the one
person of Jesus, but then, as a result of the Reformation, became
general, since now everyone through faith can participate in the
union of God with man which took place in Christ. Union with
absolute truth, however, raises man, he says, above the isolation
of his existence and makes him capable of that devotion to
general truth which opened the way to modern times.

Hegel also realized that man's freedom requires a religious
basis. Freedom only grows from participation in absolute truth,
from the human being's bond with the divine mystery of his life.
Another expression for this would be: from his likeness to God.
Freedom becomes insipid when it is cut off from this root. Then
all that remains is merely the pale formal freedom to decide this
way or that. This formal freedom becomes trivial if no substantial possibilities are attainable any more. The opinion that
one is free becomes an illusion. In this sense, Karl Marx was
right in criticizing the purely formal conception of freedom in
bourgeois democracy.

Christian theology from the beginning understood freedom
in relation to its content, as participation in the truth and life of
God, as likeness to God. Consequently it regarded the human
being who has succumbed to the transitory as unfree, even if
formally he still possessed the ability to choose this way or that.
Consequently, to be free, man needs to be set free for his true
destiny, for the freedom which lives by communion with God.
To respect in every individual human being his vocation to this
freedom means to honour the image of God in him and to respect
his mystery as a person.

The content, however, by which such freedom lives, is love.
Only the person who loves is free. Here, the ambiguous word
'love' is understood in the sense of the free, creative giving with
which the God of Jesus receives sinners, and with which Jesus
himself invited to his table those excluded from the society of
the pious and the respectable. It is the 'bestowing virtue' which
Nietzsche praised. Nietzsche, of course, no longer realized that
he was in fact glorifying the Christian idea of love. Such bestowing virtue is free from what it finds already in existence, because
it strives to change and improve it. Its operation is always

directed at least indirectly to other people, and indeed as members of humanity, even when it appears as love of truth or of a
cause, and finds expression in works of the mind or in technical
inventions. President Kennedy expressed with great feeling the
nature of this bestowing virtue in his well-known appeal to his
fellow-countrymen. 'Ask not what your country can do for you—
ask what you can do for your country'. What is meant here, of
course, is not the idolatry of false patriotism, but service of one's
own country for the benefit of humanity.

The Christian idea of love has also influenced the modern
conception of personality. Man's personal being is always
achieved in an I–You relationship, and this finds its fulfilment in
love.

The idea of the person as an I in relation to a You, was first
developed in the Christian doctrine of the Trinity. Jesus is the
Son of God only through his 'obedience' to the Father, and so,
too, the Father wills to have his being only in the generation of
the Son and by vindicating him. Only in mutual devotion to one
another and to the work of the Spirit, to the salvation of mankind, do the divine persons have their personal identity as
Father and Son. And only in the reciprocity of their love is the
Christian God a living unity.

This understanding of personality was applied to the relationship of human beings to one another in the Middle Ages, and
then again in the nineteenth century. Personality was now in
general regarded as an I–You relation. Human personal being
does not only consist in a freedom which the individual possesses
for himself alone, but finds its fulfilment only in conscious and
loving attachment to a partner. But, of course, this I–You
relation must not be misunderstood as a private relation cut off
from the context of society and mankind. Love as bestowing
virtue turns in every individual partner to humanity. It brings
into every relation to others the idea of humanity, and has in this
a standard which preserves it from any bondage to the partner.

In this way the Christian finds in Jesus the image of the God
revealed by him, the God of fatherly love. As God's image, Jesus
is the prototype of true human perfection, and every individual
human being approaches his human destiny to the extent that

his life is transformed into the likeness of the love of God revealed in Jesus' deeds, in order in that way to become truly human and truly free.

Man is not an image of God simply by nature, if we understand by that what human beings just are in any case. The destiny of man is to be truly himself in openness to the divine mystery of his life by freely giving himself to the world and to his fellow men; his destiny is his still-unachieved future which is his only from God. The longing and struggle for this coming-to-be of man as man form the hidden theme of the history of religion. In history, God and man are always manifested together, but man is so in the light of his experience of God. And where feeling for the divine mystery disappears, a distortion or at least a trivialization of the idea of man is to be expected. Consequently the religious theme cannot simply be brushed aside when man is in question.

V How is God revealed to us?

1 The presupposition: the hidden God

To ask how God is revealed to us already implies that the reality of God is not everywhere and always equally accessible. To know God is no constituent part of our natural endowment from birth, although the question of God, the question of the hidden ground of our being and of all being, incessantly disturbs us, or at all events can never completely be lost sight of, however many the disguises and distorted forms it may assume. But the answer to the question of God, which we ourselves are, the true answer, we do not find in ourselves, or in the everyday world of life around us, and the answers which men themselves give to this vital question by their myths and speculations merely blunt the radical edge of the question. God is hidden. He is neither a matter-of-fact part of the world we live in, nor its solemn complement and confirmation, as Marx thought. But since we cannot cease asking about him, we must say that God is quite unlike anything that we know.

Ancient Israel was aware of this: 'No one can see God and live' (Ex 33.20). It was quite different with the Greeks. W. F. Otto could point out as a characteristic feature of the conception of God in ancient Greece that the Greek gods had no need to be revealed, because their nature was everywhere close and familiar to men. Modern nature piety likewise needs no revelation of God, because it thinks it can everywhere directly perceive the beat of the divine pulse of Nature. The modern belief in evolution regards the progress of mankind as the all-determining power. But even where people think that from created

effects they can truly infer the being of the Creator, a revelation
of God is basically not necessary. For that kind of 'natural
theology' of the western philosophical tradition is not designed
for a supernatural complement. Its whole method is aimed at
grasping those features of the idea of God which are alone
essential.

That God is hidden has not, however, remained simply a
biblical reminiscence for the intellectually aware men of our age
in particular, for it has been experienced as an intellectual
destiny in the last hundred years more deeply than ever before.
Whereas for the Middle Ages and even for the seventeenth and
eighteenth centuries, God belonged quite as a matter of course
to the reality of the world, since Kant people have not only
doubted the possibility of proving the existence of God, but,
after Fichte's atheism controversy, have found that even the
possibility of forming so much as an idea of God has become
problematic. Ever-increasing numbers of people have come to
regard any idea of God as an empty reflection of human fears
and desires. Nietzsche's well-known dictum 'God is dead'
means primarily that the traditional idea of God of the metaphysical world-picture has come to lack credibility. All too often
we see in his words only the denial of God. But the denial
expresses the intellectual fate of the last century, for which God
has become so incomprehensible, so hidden, that people can
scarcely utter the word 'God' any more without exposing themselves to misunderstanding as if they were thinking in out-of-date
categories. It was another expression of the same intellectual destiny when, after the first World War, Rudolf Otto and Karl
Barth proclaimed God as the 'wholly other', when Luther's idea
of the hidden God was rediscovered, and almost at the same time
Karl Jaspers spoke of the Transcendence to which man is
indebted but which remains so incomprehensible to him that
even the word 'God' appears all-too-human to denote it. In the
same period, Gottfried Benn's poetry moved between the
constantly recurring question of God, and dissatisfaction with
any answer to it which the poet encountered. The evident
emotion perceptible in testimonies of this kind, which could
easily be multiplied, is, as Karl Barth acutely realized at the

time, very similar to the biblical knowledge that God is a hidden God.

It is because our time is characterized by this experience of the hidden character of God, that the question of the course of events by which his deity is revealed has assumed such decisive weight in present-day theological discussion and for many individual Christians.

2 Theophanies?

If God is usually hidden, then it would seem that revelation must be sought in special extraordinary events in which God himself appears. The oldest traditions of Israel, in fact—in an analogous way to other religions—do tell of miraculous appearances of Yahweh. These do not, however, signify what we mean by revelation in the strict sense as God's self-revelation. Self-revelation implies disclosure of actual being. A theophany, however, need not amount to that. In fact those ancient manifestations of Yahweh are wrapped in mysterious obscurity. A deity can remain unknown in essence even if it is manifested in some way. If a human being meets us, it does not necessarily mean that he discloses his very self to us. People whom we see every day can remain strangers to us. Some contact is of course made, however superficial the encounter. So, too, according to the ancient testimonies, Yahweh entered into relations with the patriarchs and Moses, in order to command the establishment of a place of worship, make important communications, express promises, or give instructions. These manifestations introduced commerce between Yahweh and Israel; henceforward Israel lived in relation with Yahweh and yet waited for him to be revealed. Moses himself, according to the priestly tradition, still had to come to know who Yahweh is, despite the manifestations that had been vouchsafed to him (Ex 6.7).

Consequently our certainty of God's deity does not depend on traditions about those initial theophanies. The revelation of the deity of the God of Israel did not take place until later. Furthermore, it is noteworthy that later biblical traditions contain fewer

and fewer mentions of direct appearances of God; there are none
at all in the New Testament. What Yahweh's manifestations
effected for Israel at the beginning of its history, the inaugura-
tion of the commerce between Yahweh and this people, is known
to us, as it already was to the early Christians, because we have
become heirs to the traditions which bear witness to that God.
This, of course, does not exempt us from the question of the
reality and the divinity of this God. It is not, for instance,
answered for us by a peremptory decision we make to regard
statements about this God as true because they are in fact found
in the Bible. Instead the question is answered by God's self-
demonstration, by his revelation.

3 God's self-demonstration by history

According to the biblical traditions, the mysterious being who in
the oldest period did not even possess a name of his own but was
designated as the God of Abraham, the Fear of Isaac, or the
Mighty One of Jacob, and then appeared to Moses as Yahweh,
showed himself to be God by the historical deeds he performed.
In what way? By the fact that the events announced in his name
in fact took place. First of all, by the miracles accomplished by
Moses in the name of Yahweh they were to recognize that behind
the man Moses there stood, not a figment of the imagination, but
a real power. When the people then trusted to this power and
went out with Moses into the desert, the greatness of the power,
which Moses called Yahweh, became clearer and clearer, and
proved favourable to the Israelites, in particular by the destruction of the pursuing Egyptians at the crossing of the Red Sea
(Ex 14.31), and then by the fact that his people did acquire a
land as Moses had promised in Yahweh's name. Could the power
which stood behind the predictions spoken in its name and so
astonishingly fulfilled, be a mere figment? Must they not go on
trusting in it as the protector of Israel? With the conquest of the
land, however, they saw confirmed not only the promise given
through Moses but the promise once made to Abraham, and so
it is not surprising that they recognized in the mysterious God of
Abraham and the God of the patriarchs in general, the same

power which with Moses was called Yahweh, and *vice versa*. And so the traditions of the patriarchs and that of Moses grew together. The exodus from Egypt and the giving of the land remained for Israel the fundamental self-demonstration of Yahweh, the proof of his power and of his will to use it for Israel. On this was based the expectation that in the future too Yahweh would maintain Israel in possession of the land, and it was the ground of the Israelites' obligation to follow the commandments announced in the name of Yahweh. The importance of the whole series of events of the exodus and conquest of the land as the basic demonstration to Israel of Yahweh's deity was expressed once again in the seventh century, a few decades before the destruction by the Babylonians of the last of the Israelite states, Judah, with a force and concision that could hardly be bettered: 'And because he loved your fathers and chose their descendants after them, and brought you out of Egypt with his own presence, by his great power, driving out before you nations greater and mightier than yourselves, to bring you in, to give you their land for an inheritance, as at this day; know therefore this day, and lay it to your heart, that the Lord is God in heaven above and on the earth beneath; there is no other. Therefore you shall keep his statutes and his commandments, which I [*scil.* Moses] command you this day, that it may go well with you, and with your children after you, and that you may prolong your days in the land which the Lord your God gives you for ever' (Deut 4.37–40).

In the exodus traditions, the formalized expression (cf. Walter Zimmerli): 'know . . . that Yahweh is God' constantly recurs. The series of events that closed with the conquest of the land was for Israel the demonstration, the revelation of the deity of Yahweh. Yet they apparently did not always see in it, as the text just quoted does, the proof that Yahweh is absolutely the only God. Even in the age of the Monarchy, it was taken for granted quite simply that other gods are in charge of other peoples and give them help (2 Kings 3.27; cf. Judg 11.24; Ps 82). And it is in fact asking too much of the events of the conquest of the land to seek in them the proof of Yahweh's uniqueness. They show indeed that a power stood behind the promises to the patriarchs and the words of Moses; but they did not yet prove that that power was the one sole power over everything. In this respect the text I have quoted runs ahead of the events.

By the collapse of Judah and the loss of the land, in the first place the self-demonstration already accomplished by Yahweh was once more called in question. It would have been refuted if it were not that for generations the prophets in the name of Yahweh had predicted a catastrophe as Yahweh's judgment on Israel and Judah, whose people had disregarded the commandments of Yahweh. The prophets' threats of calamity were now seen to be confirmed by the political collapse of the year 587, although Isaiah, for example, had probably been thinking of earlier events. Ezekiel announced the imminent disaster as a new self-demonstration of Yahweh. The content of the old formula was now reversed. To the disobedient people Yahweh reveals himself no longer as a saving power but as a destroying power (cf. Ezek 7.27; 11.12; ch. 12 *et passim*). But the prophets had also announced a new and final saving action of Yahweh, and after the collapse, Ezekiel and Deutero-Isaiah (= Is 40–55) foretold the definitive demonstration of the deity of Yahweh by the saving deed which was now to come (so Ez 37.14; Is 49.23 *et passim*). A significant change has taken place. They no longer look back to the revelation of the deity of Yahweh as an event that ended in the time of the conquest of the land, but look forward to it as coming in the future. And that is how it remained henceforward. Although the exiles returned, and Jerusalem was rebuilt, the decisive saving deed that would reveal Yahweh's deity to all peoples was more and more passionately awaited from a future that shone in colours that were increasingly those of the other world. For the apocalyptic writers it became the future of the general resurrection of the dead and of the last judgment; in the events of the last days, they foretell, not only will everything at present hidden be manifested, but also the glory of Yahweh will appear. But the manifestation of the glory of Yahweh had long meant exactly the same as self-demonstration and knowledge of his deity (Is 40.5; Ex 14.18).

If we consider the specific character of the Israelite con-

ception of revelation which I have briefly outlined, two features
in particular stand out. First, Israel understood God's revelation
as an indirect proceeding. Yahweh does not descend from heaven
in order to give a few chosen ones a special lesson about his
being and attributes, by which men are then fully supplied with
all necessary knowledge of God. Yahweh does not speak much
about himself, but acts and announces certain events. His deeds
indirectly throw light back on him. In this respect, the Israelite
conception of knowledge of God resembles in a remarkable
way that of Greek philosophy, though of course the profound
difference is at once apparent. Greek philosophy, too, sought
to come to know the being, the true form of the deity by inference
from its deeds. In this way it sought to correct the errors and
exuberant fantasies of the myths. But if Israel hoped to gain
knowledge of Yahweh from his deeds, it was not out of what is
uniformly present everywhere and always, but from unique
events, announced in the name of Yahweh and therefore produced by him, or from a series of such unique events. Consequently, for Israel the deity of Yahweh cannot be inferred
forthwith from an ever possible contemplation of the unchanging natural order, but only from quite definite events and at a
quite definite time: that is, when the events in question have
occurred and news has been received of them. Second, it is only
when the revealing events are completed that they can produce
knowledge of the deity of Yahweh as, so to speak, their last act.
This is shown in a particularly striking way by the narrative of
the passage through the Red Sea in Exodus 14: 'And Israel saw
the great work which the Lord did against the Egyptians, and
the people feared the Lord; and they believed in the Lord and in
his servant Moses' (14.31). The full significance of this fact that
the knowledge of revelation belongs to the end of the events is
apparent only in conjunction with the third point that must be
emphasized here. The power to manifest Yahweh's deity is, in
fact, not attributed only to this or that individual event, but is
increasingly ascribed to whole patterns of events. The text just
quoted from Deuteronomy chapter 4 describes the whole
history of Israel from the age of the patriarchs until the end of the
conquest of Palestine, as a single action intended to reveal the

deity of Yahweh. Even later, individual events from which Yahweh's self-demonstration is expected have their place in larger patterns of this kind. Apocalyptic, however, for the first time regarded all that happens as a single history, at the end of which the glory of Yahweh will be made manifest. Here revelation becomes the end of all events whatsoever. That is the consequence of the fact that the apocalyptic writers described the whole of world history with the whole course of its events, as the work of Yahweh. But Yahweh is to be demonstrated as the one sole God who effects everything without exception only by all history in its totality, and only right at its end.

Does this mean that apocalyptic hoped for the revelation of the deity of Yahweh only from the future? In that case, wouldn't the apocalyptic writers themselves have to remain in doubt whether Yahweh is really the one God? In fact, of course, they thought they could foresee the end in advance, and consequently the definitive revelation of the glory of Yahweh. But anticipatory vision and actual occurrence are two different things, and we have seen that to sober minds in Israel, only the actual occurrence of what had been predicted was held to demonstrate its truth.

4 God is revealed only in Jesus Christ

If we are to speak in a biblically well-founded way of Jesus Christ as the revelation of God, this has to be done on the basis of the Old Testament expectation. If the end of all history did not actually take place in Jesus of Nazareth, he would not be the revelation of God in the full sense of the word, for in that case the God of Israel, ever producing what is new, would manifest himself in ever new ways by his deeds, even after Jesus and beyond him.

But isn't that precisely the case? Hasn't history continued its course since Jesus? Didn't Jesus' announcement that the end of the world was close at hand turn out to be an historically-conditioned error? Isn't it an essential feature of every human situation in history that the end of the process of events always remains unforeseeable and that every human being goes into an open and, for him, obscure future? But if that is so, it would appear that no definitive revelation of the God who works all these ever new happenings can ever take place in history at all. Even if a God is at work behind the constant shift of events, we should have to say that he remains radically hidden for man, since man lives a life that is always incomplete in the immeasurable stream of events.

Now of course it is the case that for all of us the future is still open and at the same time hidden from us. For all human beings, that end which is not only the end of their own life but the end of all world history, has still to come. It is possible to form obscure and yet apprehensive pictures of such an end, as the apocalyptic writers did, or one may doubt whether any end of that kind awaits the world at all. Nevertheless, such doubt is only possible as long as one overlooks that the end anticipated by Jewish apocalyptic has already taken place in a human being, though, indeed, so far only in one man, Jesus of Nazareth, and that it took place in the event which became known to his disciples as his resurrection from the dead. The resurrection of the dead, of course, since the Babylonian exile had been the end of all history awaited by the Jews. If Jesus has risen from the dead to that life which is of a totally different kind from ours, if, in other words, he did not merely return for a time to this mortal life, then in him that end has already taken place, which for all other human beings down to the present is still in prospect. But in that case it has been proved that the apocalyptic expectation was not empty fantasy; for in this one man it has already been fulfilled. Consequently it is not meaningless for us others to wait for all history to end in the resurrection of the dead. This was emphasized by Paul in 1 Corinthians 15. By contemplating Jesus' resurrection, we perceive our own ultimate future. United with his teaching, actions and sufferings, we can hope eventually to share in the life which has already appeared in him. Since the end of all history which is still to come for us, already took place for Jesus at that time, nothing new beyond it has happened since, and Jesus in fact is to be regarded as the definitive self-demonstration of the God of Israel, although for the time being the end that brings fulfilment has appeared only in him and not yet in us.

By Jesus' resurrection, the God of Israel is revealed as the God with power over all that happens in history; for he who holds the end of all things in his hand, is also master of the things themselves. From the end, which is the resurrection, he is revealed as the God of the beginning also, as he 'who gives life to the dead and calls into existence the things that do not exist' (Rom 4.17). What creation out of nothing involves, can be seen by the resurrection of the dead, who of course in a radical sense no longer exist. In the event of Jesus' resurrection, however, not only the power of God but also his love for us is revealed. For Jesus' resurrection opens for those in union with him access to their goal as human beings, future life; and sin, which separates them from it, is overcome. This makes it clear that Jesus' death on the cross, as the original Christians quickly recognized, was suffered for our benefit; our own death is now no longer without hope. In all this God's love is revealed. But, of course, such a revelation of the ultimate intention and so of the innermost being of God does not mean that he becomes fully intelligible to us. No one can understand fully the wealth of what the Christ event has to say about God. After all, we have scarcely any conception of what the life of the resurrection is. We are just as incapable of thinking out how all world history, even in the history since Jesus and certainly not in the future, stands in relation to the end that has already appeared in Jesus. The sublimity and hiddenness of the God of Israel only becomes apparent in its true depth through his revelation in the life and death of Jesus.

The incomprehensibility of God precisely in his revelation, means that even for the Christian the future is still open and full of possibilities. Nevertheless, those united with Jesus have the certainty that the God of Israel, revealed in his deity by Jesus' resurrection, has power over all that happens, that nothing can separate from his love manifest in Jesus' actions and history, and that his final word, whatever form its fulfilment in us may take, is not death, but life.

The God of Israel is revealed in the full sense only in Jesus.

All earlier self-demonstrations by his action, for instance by the leading out of Egypt and the giving of the promised land to Israel, are by comparison purely provisional; they are not a definitive self-disclosure, and therefore cannot be called in a strict sense God's self-revelation. What happened in and through Jesus cannot, however, be superseded by any future events, because in him precisely the end of all things has occurred. Consequently Jesus' resurrection, and in its light the rest of his history and actions, is the one unique revelation of the deity of the one God. In fact, the very concept of self-revelation really implies that it cannot take place in manifold forms, but that if it happens at all, it can only be in a single form.

If by the special character of the events connected with Jesus, God is not hidden but wholly revealed, then he cannot be equally revealed in some other form, and the special nature of Jesus' case is not a matter of indifference as regards the revelation of God in it, but is decisive for it. That is why Karl Barth rightly repeated so constantly and emphatically that God is revealed only in Jesus Christ. But if it is only on the basis of the Christ event that it is possible to say who God is, then God's being cannot be thought of without Jesus. That is the meaning of the statement that Jesus himself is God, the Son of God and one with the Father. But the fact that the Church comes to recognize in Jesus the revelation of God, does not introduce an extraneous interpretation into Jesus' history, but ultimately belongs as the truth of this event, to the being of God himself. The Spirit of truth of this recognition is therefore once again God himself. Thus the self-revelation of God in Jesus is the root of the recognition of his deity and of the doctrine of the Trinity. The God who is revealing himself is essentially the triune God. The sole meaning of the doctrine of the Trinity is to express the being of God revealed in Jesus' resurrection. Anyone who thinks he can talk of 'God' apart from the self-demonstration of the deity of the God of Israel in the life and death and resurrection of Jesus, may regard the doctrine of the Trinity as a strange adjunct to the idea of the one God. For those, however, for whom God is everywhere so hidden that it is even doubtful whether the word 'God' is appropriate for the hidden ground of all things, the doctrine of the Trinity alone formulates the concept of the one divine being.

5 *The universality of the revelation of God in Jesus*

The prophecies of the exilic period had announced that Yahweh will manifest himself as the sole, true God, not only before the Israelites but before the eyes of all nations; both by the judgments which he executes upon them (Ezek 23 ff) and in particular by his judging and saving action in Israel (Ezek 36.23; 38.16, 23), into which, according to Deutero-Isaiah, the nations too are to be drawn (Is 49.6; cf. 45.6). Consequently no special, 'supernatural' presuppositions are necessary in order to recognize the deity of Yahweh in the events announced, only the language of the facts themselves which will take place before the eyes of all.

In this light it is understandable that the character of the Christ event as revelation inherently involved that news of it should be conveyed to the gentiles. The acknowledgment of the deity of the God of Israel by the gentile nations, is the sign of his definitive revelation, and through the Christian mission it has become a fact of world history (cf. Lk 11.29 ff).

This is the context in which the Pauline drive for universal mission is to be seen. Paul also wants to commend himself 'to every man's conscience in the sight of God by the open statement of the truth' (2 Cor 4.2). For Paul, the revelation of God is emphatically not the affair of a conventicle, but is addressed to all the world through Jesus' resurrection, which was an event that took place on the great forum of history. This event has still to be made known everywhere. Even if there are those who are blinded, who do not want to see the truth which is open and manifest (2 Cor 4.4), that makes no difference: the facts themselves preach the message announced by Paul: 'the glory of God in the face of Christ' (2 Cor 4.6).

We Christians ought surely to be the last faint-heartedly to minimize the universal truth of the revelation of God in the Christ-event, as though the facts themselves did not demonstrate

God's deity, as though a pious interpretation was needed for that. Even unbelief willingly concedes Christians the pious interpretation of an event which in itself is 'profane', provided they will admit that the same thing can 'just as well' be interpreted otherwise. But doesn't a Christian who accepts anything of the sort, himself obscure the claim of the Christian message to be the truth, and isn't that one reason why the message often sounds so powerless on our lips, so devoid of anything that might disturb? Certainly the events of Jesus' history which reveal God, and the message of these events, bring man to a knowledge which he does not have of himself. But when they are perceived in the context to which they naturally belong, that of the history of Israel, they speak their own clear language, without need of any addition. Their special character lies precisely in themselves and not in their having to be understood in a special way. The rational, unprejudiced consideration of what happened, must recognize in them the demonstration of the deity of the God of Israel. We shall see in a moment that this does not render faith superfluous. On the contrary, only through this, is its confidence well-founded.

With confidence in the universal truth of the revelation that took place in Jesus, the early Christian mission did not shrink from the question put by Greek philosophy regarding the true form of the divine; but precisely through it proved the true deity of the God who raised Jesus from the dead. But by the answer it gave, it corrected the philosophical question itself, and probably should have done so even more thoroughly than it did. For while the philosophical inquiry about God moved deductively from existing reality, understood as a cosmos of ever-identical processes and conditions, back to its origin, the biblical idea of God had opened up a more comprehensive understanding of the whole of reality as a history of ever-new events, within which the regularities of the Greek cosmos formed only a partial factor. On that basis answers have to be given to the philosophical inquiry about God which will stand up to the test of that inquiry but which would be impossible to arrive at on its basis by way of regressive inference from what is ever the same. Thus, from the point of view of the cosmic order, even the personal character of the origin as 'God' is only an anthropomorphism. The modern criticism mentioned earlier was therefore only drawing out the logical consequences of the metaphysical tradition itself. In the perspective of reality as history, however, the personal God is the only idea corresponding to objective reality, because the ever-new event makes ever-new demands on the personal decision of man, and becomes a summons to man. Besides, the fact that the conception of reality as history drawn from the biblical idea of God proves to be deeper and more comprehensive when compared with the idea of the cosmos, is itself a demonstration of the deity of the one God revealed in Jesus Christ, which is superior to that of philosophy. This still needs to be constantly shown even today in discussion with philosophy. In this, however, what is at issue is not the in itself unanswered question whether there exists any God at all, but whether the God of Israel is the one origin of all reality, and consequently truly God. Only in this way is an answer given to the question whether the source and origin actually is a God.

6 Knowledge of God and experience

According to all we have said so far, the revelation of God took place at a certain point of time, long ago. Only by way of knowledge of what happened then, is it revealed to the individual today. And here the experiences which each lives through in his own life are important. For if at that time the revelation of the one God took place for all men and times, it will also have to stand the test of men's experience of reality today.

Of course, no single experience in isolation is capable of validly convincing us of the deity of the God of Israel and of Jesus. The experience of conscience, the experience of actual guilt and the general awareness of responsibility have often been appealed to for this purpose. But this argument, a favourite one in Pietism, is inconclusive. Perhaps someone weighed down by serious guilt may be receptive to Jesus' call to penance, and perhaps accept Jesus' forgiveness. But neither is at all certain. Why should a wrong done to men lead to conversion to God, if the reality of a God is actually doubted—which was not the case with those who heard John the Baptist and Jesus? And will a conscientious person not first decline the offer of forgiveness of sins as a far too easy discharge from personal responsibility? Certainly there are people who unreflectingly grasp at any straw at all. But that is how superstition thrives, not faith. Only someone to whom the God of the Bible is already a reality will recognize not only the depth of human guilt, but Jesus' authority to forgive sins. The fact that in the light of the God of the Bible the guilt and responsibility of human life has come to be experienced to a greater depth than ever before, is indeed one sign among others that in that light all the realities of human life are clarified; and this, as we have seen, indicates the truth of the Christian revelation. Yet for this the isolated experience of conscience is not enough; it has to be the *totality* of what we are that is clarified and can enter into experience with an otherwise unattainable breadth and depth in the light of Jesus' life-history and the God revealed in him. And in this way what happened then, which is conveyed by proclamation, constantly stands the test again in the present.

The revelation event itself remains tied to the past point of time of Jesus' own life-history. Even in hearing the proclamation there is no direct experience of revelation, but only the reference to what happened then and to its validation in the present. Consequently no one needs to wait for special experiences or to work himself up into anything of the sort for God to be revealed to him; he only needs to look at what happened then and ask how it stands the test of present-day reality. In particular, the revelation of God does not mean for the individual as it were an encounter with the risen Christ, whether in private or at divine worship. How could one be secure against self-deception even then? There are no longer any such encounters. Paul names himself as the last person to have seen the risen Lord, and for Luke the time of converse between the risen Jesus and his disciples was closed with Jesus' ascension. With the exception of the first generation of disciples, all Christians live between the past of Jesus' life-history and the still unrealized future when he will return. To be sure the Spirit is present in the community in

Jesus' place, and through the Spirit, in whom we wait for Jesus'
return and our own resurrection, the risen Lord is himself
present in a certain measure. But we only know this if we are
already certain of Jesus' resurrection. Even the experience of
the Spirit is not an independent occurrence of revelation. No one
has to wait for an experience of the Spirit in order to come to
know God in Jesus. It is precisely the other way round; the
Spirit is present when anyone recognizes Jesus' life-history as a
revelation of God. Only through the Gospel of Jesus Christ and
faith in it, is the Spirit bestowed (Gal 3.2, 14).

7 Revelation and grace

The fact that the demonstration of the deity of the God of
Israel in the life-history of Jesus is a matter of insight and
knowledge, does not render faith superfluous. People do of
course say that what they know for a fact, they don't need to
believe any more. But statements of that kind are superficial in
this matter. For faith involves the participation of the believer
himself in the reality in which he believes, and this cannot be
replaced by any knowledge. Moreover, faith always has to do
with the future. The believer attaches his own future to what he
has come to recognize. Precisely for that reason faith cannot be
its own basis. Faith as pure risk would be blind credulity.
Trustful belief needs a ground on which to build. The factor of
recognition and knowledge in faith, which was formerly taken
carefully into account as ground of trust, has been all too lightly
abandoned in recent times. People think to do faith a service by
turning it into a pure risk. In reality, faith itself is undermined by
this, not least because as a faith that is ungrounded, simply
demanded and performed, it is degraded into a work of man.

The relation between knowledge of revelation and faith, is
clear from the words of Exodus 14.31 which we have referred to
several times. Because the Israelites in their wonderful deliver-
ance from their Egyptian pursuers recognize the hand of
Yahweh, they trust themselves for the future to him and to his
'servant' Moses. And when Isaiah calls upon King Ahaz to trust

in Yahweh, in a discouraging political situation, it is impossible
to overlook the fact that the person addressed lived in a history
of Yahweh's great deeds for his people and his dynasty since
David's time (Is 7.4 ff). To trust the promises of Yahweh
certainly means to live in view of a future that is still to come,
but the promise, after all, does not come to the Israelites in
isolation but always in the context of a history of deeds of
Yahweh in which his trustworthiness and might have already
been demonstrated. The prophetic statement may indeed, as in
Isaiah 7, stand in contradiction to what a superficial awareness
of the situation regards as probable, but in the context of the
divine history, its reliability is well-founded. If the proclamation of Jesus expects faith, not in the first place in himself but
trust in the God of Israel, then the history of God with Israel is
presupposed. The circumstances of faith in Jesus himself,
however, are fundamentally different before and after Easter.
Before Easter, his disciples trusted his words as men trust the
words of a prophet, that is, in hope of their future realization.
After Easter, the community trusts in him on the ground of the
demonstration given by God's raising him from the dead, that
Jesus is the bearer of the divine will for the world. If Jesus before
Easter made the final decision of the future judgment on men
dependent on their relation to him (Mk 8.38; Lk 9.26), the
community now looks forward to sharing in the life that has
already appeared in Jesus. Trust in the promised resurrection
to life is certainly opposed to what we human beings experience
in ourselves (cf. Rom 4.19 ff), but that trust is not a frivolously
accepted risk or a blind readiness to believe authority in view
of the witness of the apostles, but is grounded on Jesus' resurrection which has already occurred.

Is God only revealed to faith? Anyone who recognizes the
deity, power and love of the God of Israel by the life-history of
Jesus comes thereby to trust in him. Anyone who will not trust
himself to the God revealed in Jesus' resurrection will also
obscure for himself any recognition of the history which reveals
God, even if he once possessed it. For no one could clearly
recognize God's divinity and love and yet persist in refusing to
trust him. And so in fact only believers hold fast to the recogni-

tion of God's revelation in Jesus' resurrection. But the recognition cannot for them be a matter of a decision of faith, for that recognition is the ground of their trust in God and in Jesus Christ. And it provides the courage and spur to proclaim the truth to all men.

VI Jesus' history and ours

Christian faith is linked in a unique way with a past event. There is no other religion in which the historical person of its Founder forms the basis to such an extent that everything stands or falls with him. If we were to omit from the Christian message any account of Jesus' earthly activity and of the destiny of crucifixion and death, nothing specifically Christian would remain. In particular, the teaching of Jesus cannot in itself be the ground and content of faith. Merely as such it is by no means timelessly and universally valid. Its specific character and significance depend on the authority Jesus claimed for himself in his particular historical situation, by interpreting the Mosaic law and proclaiming the advent of God's reign with such unusual confidence. The claim implied in his teaching created the scandal which led to his execution.

Only in the light of these happenings does the peculiar shape of his teaching become clear. And not only the significance, but the validity of Jesus' teaching has its ground solely in his fate and in particular in his resurrection. For the resurrection could be understood only as the divine authentication of the man whom the Jews had rejected as a blasphemer. Without the resurrection, Jesus' interpretation of the law would have remained a gross over-statement and his announcement of the imminent end of the world would have been just an error due to the circumstances of the time. Jesus' teaching is truth, not in isolation, but only as an element in his life's destiny. Christian faith is bound up wholly and entirely with those historical events almost two thousand years ago and with their total meaning. It has no truth independently of these events. It was only through these events that the God of Israel himself showed the whole world that he was the sole true God. Hence our faith in God too is bound up

precisely with the events which constitute the life's destiny of
Jesus of Nazareth.

1 Faith and understanding

We see that Christian faith builds its hope on the truth of an
event which occurred in the far-distant past. Therefore everything naturally depends on our having a knowledge, an exact
and reliable knowledge, of these events. Faith cannot replace
that knowledge. It would have to be a reckless and desperate
faith which attempted to guarantee the reality of its ground
from its own resources. To appeal solely to the decision of faith
in answer to the question of the truth of the Christian message is
to reduce faith to nonsense. Faith presupposes a basis: something which continually proves to be true against all doubt.
That is the news of the events which together make up Jesus'
life's destiny.

The raising of Jesus from the dead has a special significance
among those events. In this connexion Paul says: 'If Christ
has not been raised, your faith is futile and you are still in your
sins. Then those also who have fallen asleep in Christ have
perished' (1 Cor 15.17 ff). The reason why such decisive importance is attached to the resurrection of Jesus is not merely
that just any individual has risen from death, but that
the person raised up is this Jesus of Nazareth whose execution
the Jews sought since he was supposed to have blasphemed God.
If this man was raised from the dead, it is evident that the God of
Israel, whom he was supposed to have blasphemed, has
acknowledged him. Our faith is based on that event. It is trust
in God who raised Jesus from the dead (Rom 4.25). The trust in
God which we call faith therefore presupposes knowledge of the
events in which the hope of our own future resurrection is
founded. That knowledge is a matter of reason. Hence in 1
Corinthians Paul adduces as a proof of the credibility of this
news the list of witnesses who have experienced the manifestations of the risen Christ.

Only from such knowledge can trust in the God who raises

the dead emerge. We must rediscover the courage to face that fact. We must learn again that faith has its presuppositions, which are not instantly to be guaranteed by a 'decision of faith', but are open to the judgment of reason. Only by re-learning that shall we cease to be over-anxious—as too many are—about our Christian identity. Then the universal truth of the event which gives life to our faith will be revealed as the truth which illuminates and perfects the world.

2 *Historical research*

How can we obtain reliable information about the fate of Jesus? How do we know that Jesus of Nazareth by his own authority proclaimed God's demands and healed sickness, and also himself announced the imminent end of the world and the advent of the reign of God? How do we know that he was apprehended as a blasphemer, executed and raised from the dead? That is something we can learn only in the same way as we get to know any other events of the past. This knowledge is not always, but may quite often—as in the case of our knowledge of Jesus—be supported by explicit accounts, human testimonies and written traditions. But no tradition can be accepted as true without examination. That would be contrary to all reason. For there is such a thing as erroneous or tendentious tradition, to say nothing of forgeries.

Anyone who reads one newspaper and occasionally compares its content with that of another newspaper knows that even true reports are always partial and necessarily selective. Facts can never be perceived and communicated except from a particular viewpoint. The influence of a specific approach on the selection and presentation is even stronger when the sole aim of the report is not to narrate the facts, but there are also other aims, as for instance the interpretation of the facts. If we have a tradition and want to get at the true state of affairs, it is not enough to decide whether we are dealing with pure forgery or conscientious reporting. We must always ask about the interest which led to the production of this particular report.

It is only by taking into account the interest really involved in each case that we can conclude to the real state of affairs.

I have tried thus to outline the procedure of historical research. It may be compared to the conduct of a criminal investigation. A good detective will not simply believe one witness or another, but will look for the signs which provide him with hints of the true state of affairs. And he will also use the statements of witnesses as such indications by drawing his own conclusions from what is said and from the fact that some things are not said. In this way the detective will reconstruct the course of events. In principle, everyone does the same thing when he wants to be certain about an incident within his own circle of personal relationships. An historian does that. But an historian needs very much more complex aids to throw light on an incident in the distant past.

The conclusions of such historical research are never completely incontestable. They are always more or less probable and can be changed by new discoveries and new approaches to the problem. Nevertheless, historically-assured certainty is the greatest certainty we can ever have of past events. If Christian faith presupposes information about events of a distant past, it can gain the greatest possible certainty about those events only by historical research.

3 Super-history?

Christian theologians today frequently dispute that the events constituting the life's destiny of Jesus of Nazareth, which are fundamental for faith, must be and can only be known by historical research. They also dispute that the conclusions of historical research must contain the ground of Christian faith. There is an overwhelming mistrust of historical research. Its application to biblical traditions seemed at one time to be leading to the destruction of the basis of faith. In particular, there are many scholars today who think that the resurrection of Jesus cannot be an historical fact. There are all-too-few analogies to an event of this kind; it is all-too-unusual for the historian to be able reasonably to assume it as a fact. Only faith, it is claimed, can venture to take such an unusual fact into consideration. But we have already seen that faith cannot guarantee the certainty of past events.

These happenings must be assumed and in fact assumed as historically certain. Christian faith would be in a bad state if the resurrection of Jesus were not really an historical fact. Moreover, as Paul insisted, our faith would be vain. But the objections against the fact of Jesus' resurrection as a real event in the past are not properly historical. They arise not so much from the character of the resurrection-accounts as from the assumption that the historian cannot accept such an unusual event as a fact. This is an unhistorical argument. The unusual character of an event is not necessarily an argument against its reality. Indeed, any event in history is more or less unique. Only if the accounts of the appearances of the risen Christ were to be explained as myths or pure legends or if they displayed unambiguously the marks of subjective visionary experiences without objective support, could the reality of Jesus' resurrection be historically contested. The mere unusualness of an event is not sufficient reason to deny its reality. Since the arguments just cited are obviously not brought forward, there is today no conclusive objection against assuming that Jesus' resurrection is an historical fact. And without this assumption it would certainly be difficult to explain the emergence of the Christian community in an historically convincing way.

Because of the apparent danger to the foundations of faith from historical research, theology has allowed itself in the last fifty years to be forced into taking a disastrous short-cut. An attempt has been made to find a sheltered area, where faith would be independent of historical investigations. Jesus' history has been described as 'super-history', 'salvation history' or 'primal history', as opposed to 'ordinary history'. New Testament scholars by and large became accustomed to speaking only of the Easter faith of the earliest community instead of the event of the resurrection of Jesus. In this connexion I shall restrict myself to the observation that there is no sort of knowledge of past events which by-passes historical knowledge. Only because

Jesus' resurrection is an historical fact has faith in the God who raised him a stable foundation. Christians must have confidence that the reality of Jesus' resurrection will constantly stand the test particularly of historical research and that historical doubt will constantly be overcome with the progress of research. But there can be no 'sheltered area' for faith. If there were, faith could not be founded on historical facts. The fact that the fate of Jesus, in which God himself is manifested, remains open to historical doubt is an essential part of the fact that Jesus was truly man.

4 The unity of history

I said at the beginning that Christian faith is wholly bound up with the life's destiny of Jesus. I have said also that in this respect it can be a question only of events which can be ascertained also by the historian. Now I must bring out the meaning of what was said more precisely from another aspect. Jesus' fate has its significance as the ground of faith, not in isolation, in itself, but within the context of the history of the people of Israel. The God of Jesus, to whom he appealed as Father, was the God of Israel; Jesus interpreted the commandments which had been handed down as the commandments of the God of Israel. Israel's expectation that the beginning of God's reign was at hand was also Jesus' expectation and the content of his message.

Jesus then, together with his message and his fate, belongs to the history in which the people of Israel from its origins was aware of being on the way with God. And this history links us moderns with the fate of Jesus. For the history of God, which began with leading Israel out of Egypt and the settlement in Palestine, did not come to an end with the resurrection of Jesus. It became from then onwards a history of the spread of the Christian faith, a history of the Christian mission. Hence the nations of the West were drawn into Israel's history of God, received from it their world-historical mission, and are still part of a history with the God of the Bible. Only in this light is the history of the West a homogeneous continuity of events, the beginnings of which are bound up with the origins of the people of Israel.

The unity of this history is founded in the unity of the God who became the God of Israel and by whom the whole history of the West is determined—whether in faith or unbelief. Therefore, whether we like it or not, we are all more closely linked with the history of Israel than—for instance—with (say) our Germanic ancestors. Only through the mediation of Christianity are we historically linked with antiquity. The European spirit is much more deeply and permanently marked by Christianity than it would seem to be at a superficial glance. Even the freedom of modern man and his technology in regard to the world is an effect of the biblical spirit: that is, a consequence of the fact that the biblical God is freely outside the world and that the world itself thus ceases to be divine. It is true that the modern age is largely characterized by the apostasy from Christianity. But even in its apostasy it has not escaped its Christian assumptions.

5 The western awareness of history

The unity of our history with the fate of Jesus in ancient Israel's history of God becomes particularly clear in the fact that the understanding of the world as a whole as history of mankind was opened up only through the Old Testament and the historical thinking which emerged from it. All other ancient religions see the world as a cosmic order, rooted in the order of the gods themselves, of which the myths give an account. For these religions earthly events are meaningful only in so far as the eternal divine order is reflected in them. It was different in Israel, the more the special character of its thinking took shape in the course of its history.

The God of Israel is not tied to a world-order, but confronts the world in freedom. God's freedom is immediately evident in the fact that he constantly brings about the emergence of what is new and unexpected. Ancient Israel, therefore, did not look to an eternal world-order but to the future which its God would bring forth. The promises of God, for which Israel lived, were directed to the future. It was solely as a result of this that time gained its irreversible direction, from promise to fulfilment. In the oldest historical books the tension of promise and fulfilment embraced only part of the events in the course of the world's history—as in the narrative describing how Solomon succeeded to David's throne. At the end, in apocalyptic literature, Israel came to see world-events as a whole as God's way to a final goal. This ultimate fulfilment was now expected as the event of the resurrection of the dead.

It is only in this light, within the framework of that conception of history, which remained as valid for the New Testament witnesses as for the later Israel, that the importance of Jesus' resurrection can be fully appreciated. The goal of all history—namely, the resurrection of the dead—has already come in Jesus, since God has raised him up. For us the end is still to come. Our resurrection has not yet taken place. For the world, history is not yet complete. This is still our situation. Here is the significance of Jesus' resurrection for us. In him the end of world-history is already accomplished: an end that awaits us also, but for us is still hidden in the future. It is only within the framework of the biblical understanding of the world as God's history directed to a final end that the meaning of Jesus' fate for our life becomes intelligible.

All Western historical thinking stems from the biblical understanding of the world as history. The modern philosophies of history have all emerged within a process of the secularization of the biblical understanding of all reality as history. Man was now to be the bearer of world-history in place of God. The unity of history was no longer to be founded in its guidance by God's providence, but in the unity of mankind continually evolving to a higher state. But if man and no longer God is to be its bearer, history is bound to lose its unity. For humanity exists only in the multiplicity of individual human beings. Once man therefore is made the bearer of history, it is impossible to hold on to any inner unity of this history. But, with the breakdown of the unity of history, we are threatened today with the complete loss of historical awareness. In the long run it is only with the God of the

Bible that the unity of the history of mankind and the heritage of our Western history are assured.

6 The truth of the hope of resurrection

Does not the biblical conception of universal history, however, presuppose the apocalyptic expectation of a general future resurrection of the dead? We have seen that this expectation forms the sole background against which the resurrection of Jesus can be seen in its full significance as the irruption of the consummation of all history. But is not an expectation of this kind—which must be counted among the anthropological presuppositions of the Christian faith—too much to demand of twentieth-century man?

I think that modern research into human nature has made it easier to see how reasonable the truth of that expectation is. Man's openness to the world, transcending any situation which arises within the world, can be understood today only in terms of the expectation of a resurrection of the dead. The expression 'openness to the world' implies that man has an infinite destiny: in a different way this was known too in former times and because of it philosophers have constantly assumed a life after death. Philosophical tradition however has understood this destiny, transcending death because infinite, as immortality of the soul.

This idea seems strange to us now, since the new anthropology has brought out the unity of all mental happenings with bodily processes and thus we are no longer able to think of a soul without a body. For this reason we can no longer conceive man's infinite destiny beyond death in terms of the immortality of the soul, but—if at all—only as a resurrection from the dead. Today then it might be possible to rediscover in an entirely fresh light the truth of the anthropological assumption of the biblical-apocalyptic conception of history: the expectation of the resurrection of the dead. Then the resurrection of Jesus ceases to appear as an unintelligible, although historically attested miracle. It then becomes intelligible again as the irruption of the consummation of history, which for us is still to come but in Jesus has already happened. Therefore our link with Jesus' fate—with his sayings, his suffering and his cross—also guarantees our future participation in what has already appeared only in Jesus: sharing in the life of the resurrection in which man's destiny reaches its consummation.

VII He will be our God

There is at the present time a marked cleavage between the world of our everyday life and the traditions which have shaped our mental attitudes towards it. This cleavage is not only typical of the relationship of Christian faith to present reality, but is particularly acute in this respect. The first reason for this situation is that scarcely any connexion can be seen between the world-picture of the sciences which determine our practical dealings with reality and the corresponding biblical ideas. Hence we can not only dispense with the God of the Bible for an understanding of nature, but methodologically it even seems more or less necessary to set aside his reality for any knowledge of nature. The same requirement arises in regard to history and the traditions which have emerged from it. It is quite generally taken for granted that, for a realistic understanding of historical facts, we must look for the motive forces behind them solely in the people involved.

In view of all this, we cannot really be surprised if no one seriously takes the reality of God into account in his working life, in daily routine and in public affairs, except perhaps for the ceremonial trimmings on festive occasions. Religion has become a private affair in which we indulge—as in other hobbies—in our spare time. In ordinary life all men and women —even Christians—largely behave as if events in nature and history, and therefore the course of events and the tasks of our times, were decided, not by the God of the Bible, but by quite different agencies.

Here we live continually and momentously against the first commandment. Nor can even drastic measures effect a change. God's commandments cannot be observed in a world which no longer has any perceptible connexion with the reality of God.

In such a world they must be thrown off as superfluous restrictions. Before we could live in accordance with God's commandments there would have to be radical changes in our whole understanding of reality. It is of course clear that this task calls for the collaboration in a special way of every Christian who helps to shape the spirit of the age.

For Israel, God—in whose name the ten commandments were solemnly proclaimed at the annual feast of the renewal of the covenant—had proved himself to be Lord of reality through the success of the exodus from Egypt, through the rescue from the Egyptian pursuers at the Red Sea and through the occupation of what had been the promised land. The Israelites were aware of the fact that they possessed the country in which they lived, not as natives, but as favourites of their God. It is only in the light of this fact that the meaning of his commandments becomes intelligible. Whether the Israelites would remain in the long run in the country granted by God or whether they would lose it again, would have to be decided by the position they took up in regard to the divine covenant-law. When they actually lost their country; when in 587 BC the Jewish upper class was deported to Babylon and Israel's independent political existence came to an end, they saw in all this, not a sign of the powerlessness of their God, but—consistently with their traditions—the result of continued infringements of Yahweh's covenant law. The commandments on the one hand presuppose the basic historical deeds which lie behind them, but on the other hand they themselves decide later history in the light of men's reaction to them.

The relationship between the history of the origins proving the divinity of God and the commandments following from this, which themselves in turn produce history, is repeated in the relationship between the Christ-revelation and the impulses of Church history and the 'Christian world' as a whole emerging from it. The revelation of the divinity of the God of Israel in the history of Jesus Christ is however different in many respects from the events to which the first commandment in the Old Testament refers and in which Yahweh proved his divinity to the Israelites.

The framework within which the Christ-history has its original meaning is from the outset—that is, in the light of Jewish apocalyptic—the whole of the world's and mankind's history. The emergence of apocalyptic awareness is closely linked with the national catastrophe of ancient Israel as a result of the Babylonian conquest of Jerusalem; with, that is, the ruin of the foundations to which the first commandment had referred. From Jeremiah and the second Isaiah the conviction emerged that God's world-dominion has passed after the fall of Jerusalem from there to Babylon, in order later to come to the Persians. The beginning of the book of Daniel is also on those lines: after the fall of Jerusalem, the mandate for world-dominion, formerly linked with the Davidic kingdom (Ps 2.8), first of all passed to Babylon. Later it was assigned to the Persians, then to the Greeks and the Hellenistic state-structures. This succession of world-kingdoms however, according to Daniel, forms merely a transitional period which will soon be superseded by a final kingdom, symbolized no longer like the world-kingdoms by animal figures, but by the figure of a man (K. Koch): the Kingdom of God himself, as it was described later, the beginning of which will be marked by a resurrection of the dead and world-judgment (Dan 12.2). Then Israel will again become the centre of divine world-dominion (Dan 7.27). Apocalyptic literature then integrated the succession of world-kingdoms as an interim period into the expectation of future salvation which rested on the predictions of the prophets, particularly from the time of the Exile.

It is only within the horizon of this universal consciousness that Jesus' entry on the scene can be understood: his proclamation of the imminence of that reign of God and of the conditions of participation in it. By consistently making men's relationship to himself—the herald of the imminent reign of God—the condition of entry into future glory, he claimed for his own part to have already anticipated the final decision and thus to be in person the definitive revelation of God. This claim of Jesus, in which many of his contemporaries could see only blasphemy, was authenticated after his execution by his resurrection from the dead and so by God himself. Thus the God of Israel is finally revealed in the history of Jesus as the one God of all men, corresponding to the apocalyptic consciousness which formed the horizon of Jesus' proclamation. In the light of the Easter-event the significance of his crucifixion as vicarious reconciliation of all men with God, in so far as they profess fellowship with Jesus, is universal just as is his claim to authority which his resurrection confirmed. This is why the world-mission came about.

As distinct from the history of the exodus from Egypt and the settlement in Palestine, which was fundamental for Israel, the new revelation of God comprised in the history of Jesus is directed to all men and not only to Israel. Through Jesus, entry into the future Kingdom of God is open to all men who put their trust in his message of its imminence. Through Jesus salvation has been brought about, not only for Israel, but for all men; reconciliation with God is effected through his vicarious suffering. But, unlike the land once promised to Israel, the salvation which took place in Jesus has to reach all men and must therefore first be proclaimed as intended for all.

In Christianity then the first commandment takes the form of a universal mission. A new light is thus thrown on the rest of the commandments: in ancient Israel their importance lay in preserving God's chosen people as a people; now they are extended to the whole of mankind. Unlike Israel, the Christian society exists only to represent mankind as a whole. The distinction lies in the fact that the Christian society must always regard its form as merely provisional if it is not to betray its universal mission: for the eschatological salvation of the resurrection-reality has already appeared only in Jesus and not yet in the rest of us. The openness of all Christian effort to the totality of a new humanity corresponds to the finality of the revelation of Christ. Universal mission and universal organization of life (which for that very reason is always provisional in its actual realization), both in the spirit of divine love uniting all things to itself, revealed in Jesus' fate, is the Christian form of the divine precepts, of life drawn from the salvation revealed in the history of Jesus.

These two features—mission and the organization of Chris-

tian life—are really two aspects of the same theme. They determine the course of history from the time of Jesus Christ. At the
same time, the history of Jesus, as anticipated occurrence of the
end in this one person, can never be superseded by any subsequent event. It is the final revelation of God. And yet the universal significance implied in it is proved by all subsequent
happenings. The God of Israel has become our God and the
God of all men through that which happened once and for all
in Jesus Christ for us and for all men. But in all subsequent
history he has proved himself constantly and to ever-new groups
of men to be who he is in the light of Jesus Christ: not however
everywhere to the same extent but in a special way to the
nations linked with Christianity in the course of time, and here
again especially to the nations of the West as to a whole culture
group marked by Christianity. The God of Israel and of Jesus
proves his divinity through his Church and Christendom, in so
far as they are obedient to their universal mission. And he
proves his divinity in judgment on Church and Christendom
when they are unfaithful to their mission.

The mission to the pagans, for which Paul cleared the way,
was the first expression of the universal mission based on the
revelation of Christ. The Jewish-Christian community, which
opted out of the mission to the pagans soon disappeared in the
course of history. The link with Greek thought, essentially
universal in orientation, was part of the inner logic of the
mission to the pagans. First, in the encounter with expectations
of redemption which had apparently developed at many points
simultaneously with the Hellenization of ancient Eastern
religions. That was how the Greek philosophical tradition,
especially of the philosophical question of the true God, came
to be accepted. We should not be misled into thinking that the
ancient Hellenistic heritage was thrust on the early Church as
something alien, still less as a falsification of the Gospel. Its
appropriation followed necessarily from the universal nature of
the Christian message and is not to be separated from the foundation of the Church. If the Christian message had not recapitula-
ted the longing for redemption found in the piety of the mystery
religions at that time, it would have been unable either to

develop or to take root. If biblical monotheism—now freed from the particularist Israelite-Jewish claims—had not been linked with the philosophical question of the one true God, the God of Israel would never have been accepted in faith by non-Jews as the one God of all men. The universal mission was made possible not least by the absorption of the Mediterranean world in the Roman Empire. Those are the foundations of Christianity; if it denied them, Christianity would betray its true nature and become an insignificant sect.

The Constantinian turning-point of the fourth century, the emergence of a Christian emperorship, is also related in a wholly positive way to the revelation of Christ. Today we like to talk of the end of the Constantinian age and turn away hastily from the idea of a union of Church and state. But the revelation of Christ is by no means alien to the legal sphere or—therefore—to that of the state. As the Old Testament community was essentially a legal fellowship—a legal fellowship within the people of Israel, chosen by Yahweh and organized by his commandments—so the New Testament community is essentially a legal fellowship, oriented to the eschatological legal fellowship, but now in such a way that it embraces in principle the whole inhabited world.

It was not without reason that Jesus interpreted and practised God's law and by that very fact acted as king of the end-time in whom the Kingdom of God is present. His community does not live yet in the age of the perfect reign of God, but it is nevertheless constructed in the expectation of God's Kingdom and in fact in anticipated sharing in this. It was in that spirit that the primitive Christian mission was able to adopt ancient ethics. On those lines the early Church did not fail to seize the opportunity of closer association with political life when a Christian emperor appeared in the person of Constantine. In a similar situation the Church would constantly have to make a similar decision and it could not of itself again shift off its share of responsibility for the political world. It could not adopt the escapist attitude of Gnosticism. Of course the serious problems of a Christian state immediately became clear, not only in the question of military service for Christians, but especially in the fact that the provisional character of all political organization began to be overlooked: the dead weight of the ancient Roman empire loomed large and even the pagan imperial cult was largely maintained under different auspices.

The distinction between Christian empire and God's Kingdom, thus also that between the empire and the Church in quest of the Kingdom of God, became blurred. The result was that the universal mission came to a standstill, since Christianity and Roman emperorship had been blended into a unity. Moreover, just as the provisional character of the organization of Christian life was lost sight of, so too the provisional character of dogmatic formularies was overlooked. Hence, in opposition to the imperial uniformity of faith, there emerged the great schisms of the ancient Church, the result of which was that Syria, Palestine and Egypt later easily became a prey to Islam.

We may look for God's guidance not only in the rise of the Constantinian empire but in developments in the West, in the consolidation of papal power in the midst of the chaos of the migration of peoples; in the conversion of the European peoples to Christianity; and in the emergence of the Western emperorship of Charlemagne. In the tragic conflicts between papacy and empire we shall see the failure to appreciate the provisional character of the forms of Church and society. The defeat of the imperial power affected also the papacy itself and the result was a complete breakdown of any universal consciousness: the rise of the idea of the national state which had largely emancipated itself from Christian impulses. The effects of the uninhibited pressure-group politics of the Italian city-states of the thirteenth century, utterly regardless of Christendom as a whole, and the narrow-mindedness of a Western Christianity regarding itself as alone orthodox but still able to command allegiance, were demonstrated by the Fourth Crusade which sealed the final break between East and West and brought about the collapse of the Byzantine bulwark against Islam.

Not only the struggles between emperor and pope but the whole dogmatic-juridical organization of the medieval Church revealed the absence of any critical awareness of the distance from the *eschaton*, from the final end of the world. The same thing became evident again in the way the Roman Church ruled out the Reformation. On the other hand the failure of scholasticism to assimilate the ancient intellectual heritage into Christianity led to the extensive intellectual crisis of modern times, which oddly enough was accelerated by the turning of originally Christian impulses against the Church and its theology.

Right up to the self-slaughter of the 'Christian family of nations' in the European wars of the last centuries, up to the failure of creative love in the age of early capitalism, and the neglect of opportunities in regard to the nations outside Europe who are now turning the national idea against Europe: up to all this Western history in the age of colonization is a story of human greed and divine judgment, but also constantly of divine preservation. As a result of the Enlightenment—of all things—Europe was preserved as a spiritual unity despite denominational conflicts. Western civilization and the Christian heresy of Communism have spread more successfully throughout the world than the missions of the Churches. Here too there are opportunities for a Christianization of their mission.

God pursued his aim of a universal Christian mission through the West and it is from Europe particularly in modern times that the world has grown into a unity; not however through the spread of the Christian faith, but indirectly by way of Western science and technology, which themselves emerged from the intellectual background of Christianity. God can also bring this world, as it becomes more closely united nearer to his own goal, the knowledge of the truth of Christ. We do not know whether the West can still serve him in this respect as instrument and centre, when it has so often forfeited its historical chances. But as heirs of its traditions we are still summoned to proclaim to all men the universal truth of the revelation of Christ.

That remains God's first commandment, set before us as the law of our own history, rooted in the history of Jesus Christ himself, constantly confirmed by the experiences of divine guidance and judgment in the history of Christendom. Our history is full of proofs that the God of Israel is our God, with the intention of being the God of all men. This requires us in all fields to live our life in his light, looking to a new unity of the

Church, to new forms of the unification of mankind through creative love and to the knowledge of all reality as his creation, humbly aware that we are not yet at the eschatological goal but still courageously shaping our life and our world to witness to the truth of Christ. For this we are certain of God's help and in it our life will find fulfilment.

VIII Divine revelation and modern history

Nowadays it is no longer self-obvious that God has anything at all to do with history as we experience it. Some theologians and other Christians see the events of human history as occurring so to speak on some plane other than divine revelation. To be sure, we believe that God as the Creator effects everything that happens, and that unless he willed it not a hair would fall from our heads. But this dimension of history seems to some so obscure, that in events we experience, or in those reconstructed according to testimony from the past, we are quite unable to find any connexion with the revelation of God in Jesus Christ. Divine revelation can seem to be an event that breaks into our world vertically, from above, and consequently cannot be named in the same breath as all those events which occur on the horizontal surface of our history.

1 Revelation and history—are they opposed?

This opposition of revelation and history was characteristic of the theological theory of culture after the first World War. It now needs to be revised. Of course God is quite distinct from the world; he is unutterably different from it. But insofar as he reveals himself, he is in the world. That, in fact, *is* history: that God makes himself manifest in the world. History is God acting in his creation. Therefore history cannot be fully understood without God. And it is not understood at all if it is conceived as the field of human action alone. In themselves, human actions are no more than elements of history but not as yet what makes

their course (or even large sections of their course) a whole.
It is by no means accidental that the understanding of reality
as a whole, as a continuously changing course of history, first
arose in the people of Israel, under the impact of the God of
Scripture in his almighty action. Whereas the God of the Bible
encompasses his creation in his almighty freedom, the unity of
that creation is that of a history in which something unforesee-
ably and unpredictably new is continually happening from
beginning to end. Through the whole course of his action in this
history, from the beginning to the end of creation, the biblical
God reveals himself as the Lord of the world, as the true God, as
the Creator who remains in control of his work. Ultimately, that
becomes obvious only at the end of all human history when all
occurrence is completed and can be seen as a whole. Only from
that end is it possible to decide what meaning is ultimately to be
attributed to all that has gone before. As long as unpredictable
events can still happen, it is also possible for all that has already
happened to appear in an entirely new light. For that reason the
Bible has expected God's final revelation and the associated
final elucidation of everything that has happened in the world
as something that will occur in the ultimate future which is to
bring the end of the old world and the renewal of creation.
Therefore the ultimate revelation is something which occurs at
the end, because it has to do with occurrence as a whole, and
because it is only through occurrence as a whole that the God of
the Bible can declare himself in his divinity, as the Lord of all
things. Occurrence is a whole only when it has come to an end.
Therefore the history of Jesus can only count as divine revelation insofar as in it the end and that which is ultimately valid is
already present in advance, in the midst of a time which is not
yet concluded. If the biblical conception of divine revelation is
rightly to be understood thus, then it is impossible to talk about
God's revelation in any other way than historically: and that
means conceiving history as a whole, as world history, as far as
that is possible in the present state of our experience and
knowledge.

The fact that our knowledge of history is always inadequate
and full of gaps is no argument against that. Our knowledge of

the meaning of revelation is also inadequate. But that does not mean that it is insignificant. We can only try to speak in a very provisional way of the Christ revelation in the context of world history with which it is essentially linked. Yet that is the one and only way in which here, on the path of our earthly pilgrimage, we can speak appropriately of divine revelation in Jesus Christ.

If we recognize the close association of revelation and history and try to see the Christ revelation in terms of its actual connexion with world history, then we can live and act as Christians in our particular historical situation without any break. We do not have to switch to another system when we are concerned with the actual demands of our historical circumstances and the decisions to be made within them. The difficulty of Christian ethics today is that apparently we have to act on two quite distinct levels, and must jump from that of Christian faith onto that appropriate to the actual situation, in order to act at all; just as, on the other hand, we might be thought to have to jump back out of the so-called natural experience of reality in order to enter into the condition of faith. The reason for that kind of transition disappears once we have understood the inner association of revelation and history. Even modern history, from which the situations of our own present activity are derived, is then encompassed by divine revelation.

Modern history is not however divine revelation so to speak of itself. The connexion between revelation and history is not to be taken in the sense that revelation is necessarily to be encountered wherever one gains entry to history. Yet the revelation of the divinity of the biblical God has to do with history as a whole. It is disclosed only in history as a whole; not uniformly in every specific event, but only—as we have seen—in an end-perspective. For history is a whole only when seen from the end and through that end. Since the end is for us something still to come, it is sensible to ask whether history can in fact be a whole for us. We Christians can only answer Yes, because in Jesus Christ the end of all events and therefore that which is ultimately valid and meaningful has already pre-occurred; that which is still open future for us, into which we are still entering, has already made its appearance in him.

The specific nature of the history of Jesus is to be ultimate in that way. Hence this special event makes what is otherwise unconcluded history into a whole. History partakes of the nature of revelation only in terms of its end as it has appeared in Jesus Christ. Not of itself, but only from Jesus and towards him do the epochs and all the individual instances of history take part in divine revelation. Only thus do they share in and help to show God's divinity.

Therefore we inquire into the light which shines from Jesus on history as a whole insofar as he is the end of history that has already occurred and therefore first and foremost makes all that has happened a whole, makes it world history. We ask especially what kind of light Jesus Christ sheds on modern history, for he is the goal and the end of all history. We ask that in order to discover our own place, the location of our activity in God's history as a whole. In so doing we cannot of course look at modern history as something detached. We have to see modern history in the context of the history of Christianity as it has proceeded from Jesus. That is the only way to conceive appropriately its historical connexion with Jesus Christ himself.

I shall confine myself to only a few further indications in this respect. A detailed exposition of Christianity in late antiquity and the Middle Ages is not my task here. It should be enough to set forth a fundamental viewpoint and describe its application to ecclesiastical, political and spiritual life.

2 Universality and anticipation

The fundamental viewpoint to which I have just referred is the interweaving of universality and anticipation or provisionality, which is characteristic of all Christian formation of life insofar as Christian life is shaped by acknowledgment of Jesus Christ as God's revelation.

(a) *Universality:* Testimony has to be given of the revelation of the one God of all men and of all times. Revelation aims at the recognition of all men and at their life in all areas of reality. But that universality of the Christ revelation can take form in

Christian life only in a provisional manner. The final deter-
mination of creation, life out of death, which already appeared in
Jesus through his resurrection from the dead, has not yet made its
appearance in us. Therefore everything which we do as individuals and together in community can have no more than a
provisional significance. The Christian life-formation is
necessary because the God who is revealed in Jesus Christ is the
creator who claims our life and the world as his own. That
Christian life-formation is however continually being made out
of date, because the creation is not yet concluded. All Christian
life-formation runs the permanent danger of forgetting its own
provisionality. At the same time however this provisionality
makes it clear why even in a society formed by Christians, a
church organization has to persist alongside the state. The
Church recalls the future salvation towards which Christians live
their lives, beyond all present actuality. Nevertheless, it is
possible for the Church to forget the temporary nature of its
forms of life and to understand itself as the possessor of salvation,
as the germ cell of the Kingdom of God, instead of as the advance
guard of those who are directed to the coming of that Kingdom.

But in saying that I am already applying our fundamental
viewpoint. *First* let us look at the cultural and historical aspect.
The universality of the Christian message and of the God of the
Bible ordained the reception by the early Church of Greek
thought (and above all Greek philosophy), which was universal
in itself. Of course it did so in very different ways. For
the present context, it suffices to remark that Greek thought
was, of necessity, profoundly altered by Christianity. For its
own part, Greek philosophy was unaware of its own historicity
and provisionality, and in fact tried to grasp what was always
and timelessly true. But the Christian transformation of the
Greek heritage was itself only provisionally successful, and even
now is inconclusive.

Second: The universality of the Christ revelation is closely
connected with the just life. The God of the Old Testament was
in a very special way a God of Justice, and the Kingdom of God
awaited by Israel and proclaimed by Jesus is primarily the
ultimate establishment of justice in humankind as a whole.

For that reason, the Christian Church could not remain unin-
terested and take no part in the political and legal community
in which it lived. In the Holy Roman Empire since Constantine,
for instance, it was possible for what was intended to be a
universal political community of the inhabited earth to arise
under Christian leadership. This process was essentially
appropriate to the context I have already described. The Christian religion is by no means unworldly. Of course the way in
which the universal policy came into being as a Christian
empire on the basis of the Roman Empire was wholly time-
conditioned and alterable. The denial of the provisional
nature of the Christian structure of life in this political area
was a particular danger and in fact contributed to the ambiguity
of Constantine as an historical figure.

Third: In contradistinction to all provisional Christian world
structures, the Church remains the community of those who
hope for God's future from a basis of belief in Jesus Christ. The
Church too is universal by nature. The Church of the one God
and his one agent of revelation can only be a unique, universal,
catholic Church, as Protestants also acknowledge in the
Apostles' Creed. This unity of the Church has been expressed
in various ways. In the West it has been shown increasingly in
the form of one head, in the primacy of the Bishop of Rome. To a
certain degree, in the sense of a primacy of honour, this development was recognized by eastern Christianity. It is not to be ruled
out from the start as a deviation. But the development of the
Papacy has gone beyond the position of a *primus inter pares*
to become something approaching an absolute monarchy in the
Church. Here again the provisionality of the ecclesiastical form
of life has been neglected, as well as, at certain times, its
difference from state goals and methods.

The foregoing has at least indicated the requisite bases of a
theological approach to modern history. It is not my task to
delineate the course of modern history itself. Even a sketchy
account would go far beyond the bounds of this chapter. In
addition, modern history includes too many processes which cannot be brought into one and the same line and which are nevertheless reciprocally involved to such a degree that they have

codetermined the whole. I shall mention only a few aspects which have become characteristic and determinative of modern times so that their significance applies not only to a single epoch but to the course of modern history right up to the present day. I think of the triumph and the transformation of the national idea, of the division of western Christianity, of the secularization of European culture, of the transformation of our world by capitalism and industrialization, of the evolution of a democratic political life and finally of the changes in the relation of Europe to the rest of the world.

3 The national idea

In modern times nationalism has suppressed the old universalism of the Christian *imperium*. The Christian Roman empire as it was renewed in the west by Charlemagne and his German successors in the Middle Ages under quite different historical conditions has probably always been more of a dream than a political reality, even though politically a very effective dream. It was never able to establish its authority throughout Europe. Within, its universalism was contradicted by the dynastic interests of the great feudal lords, and to some extent by the special dynastic interests of the Emperor himself. Without, and on the peripheries of its area, it soon came into conflict with national impulses. In England and in France, it would seem that the royal dynasties were associated with national feeling at a relatively early date. In France it flared up after the Battle of Bouvines in 1214 and found a symbolic figure in Joan of Arc during the Hundred Years War. In England it developed after the reforms under Henry II and Edward I. In the fourteenth century a national feeling evolved in Italy (not without French influence) that extended beyond the narrow borders of the Italian states. It was closely connected with the rise of the vernacular and found eloquent expression in Petrarch's *Italia mia*. Language was also immensely important for the later development of a German national feeling and for the rôle of the Reformation. The fact that a national consciousness developed relatively late in Germany (not without a reaction against the French and Italian contempt for 'barbaric' German) is not astonishing in view of the special association of Germany with the supra-national institution of the Empire. The rise of nationalism meant too that the Holy Roman Empire was seen from without, but also henceforth in Germany, as a national concern of the Germans—certainly, at least, by the Emperors themselves. One might almost say that that other universal Christian institution, the Papacy, became in the Renaissance period no less fundamentally an Italian national concern.

The decline of the Empire and the Papacy as universal institutions after their tussles in the high Middle Ages was very fateful for Christianity, since the national idea, which in any case repressed universalist thinking in the political area, did not have its roots in Christianity. The fall in imperial power, which was sealed in Germany with the Thirty Years War, left behind a vacuum. The old idea of a Christian family of nations could not fill that vacuum, not only on account of the denominational differences which had arisen in the meantime, but mainly because national feeling justified reasons of state as the highest consideration in political life. That meant that Christianity ceased to be the ultimate yardstick for political conduct. The union of François I with the Turks (whose capture of Constantinople and the Balkans had so shocked Christendom) against the Emperor Charles V, showed the new situation as it was.

The rise of the national ideal did not prove a blessing for the European nations. From now on the struggle for hegemony or a balance of power kept Europe in continual suspense. That did not change éven when with the French Revolution the national idea received a new emphasis in the opposition of popular sovereignty and princely rule. Only now came the rise of modern nationalism, first of all in the France of the revolutionary wars. In the Napoleonic wars it awakened corresponding passions among the other nations. The national liberals of the 1848 Revolutions were still able to hope that the formation of national states would also secure peace between peoples who until then had been led by their mónarchs into unpopular wars. Subsequent years showed however that the difference between monarchy and republic made hardly any difference as far as peace between nations was concerned, and that the national passions of the masses could be more lethal than the honour of princes.

The Germans have had especially unfortunate experiences with national ideals. It should be easier for Germans to discard them than it is for others. Germany managed most of the time to avoid the pressure of the national idea, being initially affected by the universal Empire and then by small dynastic states. The difficulties attending the attempt to forge a German national state out of the results of that process were experienced by the Frankfurt Parliament of 1848 with its oscillation between greater German and small-scale German solutions. The Bismarckian Empire was to a great extent a compromise between national and Prussian interests. The unthinking attempt to make it one of the most significant of the older national states, and blind trust in its own national power, led Germany into that isolation which contributed so much to the outbreak of the first World War, and the national resentment which the Versailles Treaty aroused together with the great world crisis made possible the rise of Hitler, the excessive German nationalism of the Third Reich, and the second World War and the consequent collapse. If Germany had been less preoccupied with national fever, then perhaps it would have been able to continue as a national state. But too much was sacrificed on its altars, and the destruction of the German national polity had to be accepted as the result of that behaviour.

German national demands for the 1937 borders seem, given that situation, impenitent. Community of West Germans with the Germans of the Democratic Republic is attainable only within the framework of supra-national agreements. To be quite clear about all this means rejecting the national idea as a definitive political yardstick. The German tasks of the present lie in the formation and confirmation of supra-national communities, in which the specific national mode can persist only as a subordinate element. That is already evident in western Europe. That a conjunction of nations should occur not only first and foremost on the basis of a world organization but in the small circumference of a common history, is so sensible that we have to ask why it didn't happen long ago. The European union must of course stay open to the outside world, to the nations of the Americas and to those of eastern Europe. Perhaps the one time moat between us and the latter is not so deep now as it seems, and the weight of a long history in common may prevail in regard to western Europe, in Russia and in the Balkan states more effectively than the frontlines of present politics would lead us to suppose. It is quite obvious that in regard to Germany's eastern neighbours, only a retreat from national thinking can lead to a lessening of reciprocal tensions and to a permanent long-term understanding. In a really decisive move towards supra-national thinking the tradition of Christian universalism which has been broken since the end of the medieval Empire and suppressed by national dynastic thought, can become effective in a new way.

4 The division in the western Church

The second aspect of modern history which is relevant to the present discussion is the division in the western Church with its profound consequences in all areas of life of the western nations. The universal empire and the universal Church were not just rivals in the Middle Ages but went together. It has often been noted that the victory of the Popes over the Hohenstaufens also started the decline of the Papacy. The period that followed was one of a dependence of national interests first on France, then on Italian politics, interests which were much more alien to the Papacy than the Christian universalism of the Emperors. The conciliar Party in the time of the Reformation Councils was also dedicated to the principle of nationalities, so that the independence of the Papacy seemed to be made possible only by means of curial centralism, when the Popes themselves no longer saw themselves as monarchs but as the first bishops of Christendom. With a papal centralism of that kind, the Reformation occurred.

The Reformation did not happen suddenly but gradually, through the exclusion of Luther's attempts at reform from the

Roman Church and by Luther's insistence on his convictions. The latter was possible only because of the late medieval subordination of interpretation by the magisterium of the Church to the authority of Scripture. That was how Luther's cause obtained its power of conviction. Without it his cause could not have survived; nor could it have done so without the territorial constitution of the sixteenth century which Luther protected from the direct attack of his opponents, together with the warlike procedure of Charles V, the anti-Roman mood in Germany, and much else. The official Church would not allow itself to be reminded by Luther of the provisional nature of its structure and its customs, but reacted with the force of the *status quo*. In so doing it lacked true catholic breadth; Luther, having begun with the questions of penance and indulgences, had to go much further than he originally intended, right up to the formation of a separate church organization. The progressive element in this course of events, and the way in which things were forced ahead by a number of accidents, make it impossible to set Protestantism against Catholicism as another religion; as, so to speak, a religion of conscience against Catholic sacramental piety. Such oppositions, which were general not so long ago, are used to justify a split which as such was sheer misfortune, being no less separative than the division of Western from Eastern Christendom. If one looks at things from the viewpoint of the nature of the Church, which can only be one, it is impossible to accept that division. However convinced we are of the justice of Luther's action in his situation then, we must do everything we can to move beyond those circumstances. It is shocking that in spite of numberless changes, and in spite of a remarkable growth in reciprocal understanding, that situation has persisted in the Papacy's self-understanding right up to the present. What needs to be opposed is not a primacy of honour of the Papacy in the midst of the company of Christian bishops, in the sense say of the early Church, but the monarchistic, centralistic Papacy, which appears to stand in the way of reformability of the Church. Such an understanding of the Papacy means a denial of the provisional nature of all ecclesiastical forms of life, even of dogmatic formulations, as opposed to the ultimate future of Jesus Christ. We must hope that this is not the true shape of the Catholic

Church itself, that in that Church, too, humble insight into the provisional nature of its own form is alive and effective. Then, to an increasing extent, cooperation will become possible, perhaps tentatively at first, just as it already takes place between other churches in the World Council of Churches, and thereby an increasing degree of mutual recognition in spite of all the differences that remain. Christianity must learn to live with pluralism in its own ranks, in order to adjust appropriately to the pluralism of modern society. Perhaps the only way for the unity of Christians to take new shape is in this unpretentious and hard way. The inevitability of this way and the extent to which we still have to worry about the division of the churches can be seen from its results in the history of modern times. The last upsurge of the Empire under Charles V was inconclusive. The denominational oppositions led to denominational wars which had especially devastating effects in France and Germany. At the end of this period, people were tired of confessional sides and that situation favoured the beginning of alienation from ecclesiastical Christianity. The denominational opposition had the inescapable effect of relativizing the Christian message itself, as proclaimed through the Churches, as far as men were aware. There was not just the one form of Christianity but another, and then others. That had of course a particularly pernicious effect in the mission field. Imagine for a moment the leading position of modern Europe in a world without a divided Christianity; that will give some idea of how difficult the missionary task has been made by that very division. The successes of missionary endeavours are then all the more astonishing. At the same time, within and without the old Christian territories, new and living adversaries of Christian faith have arisen. The confrontation with them is something that Christianity will hardly be able to survive if it is not united.

5 Secularization of European culture

The next three aspects of modern history need only be touched on. The first is the secularization of European culture. I have already mentioned its connexion with the division of the churches, which is of course not its only cause. The growing tendency to a separate national life also favoured the development of a secular culture. This process, which is characteristic of the modern as distinct from the medieval era, has however two aspects. It does not necessarily imply dechristianization, but primarily only a form of life which is appropriate to reality but with roots in the Christian belief in creation and in men's commission to rule over the earth. The naturalism of the Renaissance and its defence of active life in the world against the old idea of contempt for the world do not seem as a whole to have gone so far from Christianity as people tended to believe in the nineteenth century. The emphasis on the *vita activa* had its counterpart in the reformation work ethic. Only the seventeenth-century transition in naturalism to a non-historic mode of thought made alienation from Christianity unavoidable. A precondition for that transition was already present in embryo in the Christian thought of the high Middle Ages; in, that is, the divorce between the natural and the supernatural in thirteenth-century scholasticism. A specifically Christian concentration on the supernatural makes the way seem open for further autonomization of the natural. This distinction originally expressed the compromise of theology with the incursion of Aristotelian philosophy. The various approaches of modern thought, which were in fact much closer to the spirit of Christianity, in the natural sciences for example, were not used to redress that distinction. Instead they had to oppose an ecclesiastically approved Aristotelianism. After the Thirty Years War there was a general understanding about confessional barriers in the area of the natural. In the beginning of this alienation from Christianity, above all as it had developed historically, and fatefully, in the form of a split between denominations, we can see the effects of the reformation divide. That trend to dechristianization is possibly reversible even now, though of course we cannot reverse the secularization which preceded it. The new secularization of modern life and thought has instead to be made conscious of its Christian roots. That is the only chance of arresting dechristianization. Secularization is no more than a continuance of the provisional, and cannot therefore have the last word. But the universalism of faith in creation demands a positive appraisal from us; and as the arena of the provisional the world is the place appropriate to our situation, so long as we realize the temporary nature of the life we lead in it.

6 *The development of capitalism into industrial society*

In modern times capitalism became industrial society. The immense relevance to modern history of that development cannot be discussed here in detail. But it is an enormously problematic topic as soon as we try to examine it theologically. The Church stood in the way of emergent capitalism by reason of its ban on interest and above all by its traditional criticism of riches. In the course of secularization even the wealth of the Renaissance was defended—as an opportunity for the exercise of virtue. Even the Protestant ethic made a major contribution to the rise of the capitalist spirit, for economic success was seen as a confirmation of Christian vocation. The alteration of the whole structure of society by industrial capitalism was hardly evident before the end of the eighteenth century, when the private form of capitalist economy became problematic. The significance of industrialization for society as a whole made it a concern of society as a whole—a political concern. That was more or less universal from the beginning of the nineteenth century. The difference in the form of property, whether private or communal, hardly decided that development. Much more decisive, so it would seem, was the fact that the major problems of the industrial organization of society are political problems, and as such cannot be left to themselves but have to be taken by society as a whole as its own responsibilities. That accords with the relation between the Protestant work ethic and the communal well-being subserved by the individual vocation. In modern times parliamentary democracy has come into being as a basis for the political task of equalization of interests.

7 Parliamentary democracy

In order to grasp the democratic form of state adequately, we have to consider its historical roots in British parliamentary institutions. It is very easy to criticize the democratic principle. The function of democratic institutions in regard to historical growth is an obvious problem. The co-responsibility of the nation for the regime (something which developed through the extension of the activity of the House of Commons, above all in the Tudor sixteenth century) was a great legal achievement. Christian and Stoic motives mingled in its further development into democracy. The Stoic heritage of democracy—the principle of equality and the sovereignty of the people (to be found even in the Magna Carta of 1215)—contains hidden dangers, especially in the majority principle. In fact men are not equal, neither in judgmental capacity nor in their social function; and justice is not seldom perceived and grasped only by a minority. That finding of course speaks against the principle of majority. It is possible to understand the tenacious hold of the monarchic principle in Christian Europe, on the basis of Christian tradition, in particular by reason of its acknowledgment of the sinfulness of man.

The democratic ideology which won such power over sympathetic hearts in the eighteenth century has persisted in an inchoate, immature and problematic condition to this day. The dominance of its Stoic elements, and that especially of an abstract notion of equality, was not accidentally associated with a non-historical, technical understanding of the ideal state of human society. In actuality, however, democratic institutions have become instruments of an equalization of interests without which modern society would be inconceivable. They alone would seem to make it possible nowadays for a regime to surrender power peacefully.

Even if the advantages of a democratic social order are primarily pragmatic at the moment, the tradition of democratic ideas is capable of fruitful extension from its Christian beginnings—which deserve more emphasis than the Stoic and natural-law elements. In this connexion, freedom is to be understood not in the sense of individualistic self-will but essentially in the sense of human dignity; similarly, equality is to be understood as the equal dignity of each man or woman before God. The inevitable, naturally-conditioned inequalities are not however to be by-passed but have to be expressed in distinctive social rôles and ordered in a suitably complementary manner. That equality is primarily to be understood as equality before God is important, for it has to take effect as a corrective and not as a constitutive principle of social relations. If misused for the latter end, equality will always assume an ideological character for the very reason that it is unrealizable as complete equality. What is more, the total equalization of reciprocal human relations would dissolve all community, for a sense of community is possible only between unequal though complementary partners. The Christian element in the origin of democratic principles is most important, perhaps, as a stimulus to free initiative which, in contradistinction to the tendency to equalization, is the positive precondition for egalitarian thinking in the adaptability of political organization to social change. This accords with the dynamics of modern history and especially the world-openness of man, and also the ultimately effective tendencies of democratic societies to assimilate nations and unite them in supra-national institutions.

In regard to attempts progressively to limit and constitutionally check any exercise of power, whether economic or political (claimed in the name of the majority), the democratic social order is probably closer than any other currently feasible to a form of life which is provisional and therefore alterable and only partially valid—when seen, that is, in the light of an eschatological human destiny that will never be achieved in this world.

8 Europe and the rest of the world

The period since 1500 has been seen as the era of the expansive West. That expansion took the form of colonial acquisitions and an associated spread of western languages and political and cultural institutions over the entire globe. It is still very difficult to offer a balanced judgment on the positive achievements and the inadequacies and sins of the colonial era. Whereas nationalism in the former colonial nations tends now to stress the exploitation and repression that took place in colonial times, we must remember that Europeans also perceived the civilizing of subject peoples as a task and duty which they duly undertook. Christian missions justifiably helped the process; for what was exported from Europe to Africa and Asia was for the most part received as a whole; the process largely took place on a basis of Christianity. Perhaps the civilizing effects of the colonial era are only now reaching their high point, when the political dependence of the colonial territories is largely at an end, and, emulating the nationalism of the white nations, they can make their achievements more lastingly their own. For a long time, of course, Europe did not undertake its tasks in Asia and Africa with true high seriousness, and had to give them up abruptly after the two World Wars. This rapid loss of its universal stage was the consequence of Europe's national self-dismemberment, a process indirectly and directly conditioned by the rise of Communist Russia and its influence on the world situation. It is characteristic of the present situation that the civilizing achievements of the West are adopted much more readily than their cultural foundations. That need not have been the case; and a consequence for the non-European nations is the hard task of making the European and American influence on their ways of life gell with their own traditions. One result, however (as the Renaissance of Hinduism in India shows), is an approximation to European and Christian thought. What we have here is to a great extent a kind of indirect and rudimentary mission— evidence in fact of much more impressive successes than the actual missionary work of the churches. Nevertheless it could perhaps be a starting-point for the 'real' mission. The spread of Marxism in Asia and Africa also has to be seen in the context of that indirect mission. For Marxism is in many respects a Christian heresy, even though it may be turned to anti-Christian ends. Its secularized hope in the future will eventually declare its illusory nature, revealing however that longing for the true hope of the future which the Christian gospel brings.

I have mentioned some aspects of human achievements in the period of modern European history in the light of the responsibility laid on the nations of Europe by divine revelation in Jesus Christ. That responsibility has been present since the Christian message was passed to the nations of Europe and through them to others, especially those of the American continent. It cannot be rejected. Because that is the case, the history of the West in all its stages can be seen as a history whose Lord is the God of the Bible. He receives into his service the men and women of the areas where the Christian message has taken hold and uses them as his instruments in a more direct and less mysterious way than elsewhere in the world, because he does so within the context of Christian tradition. That is the case even where men openly or secretly oppose him, as has happened so often in modern European history. But, in spite of all such opposition, it is clear that ultimately God, and not the men whom he makes his partners, is the mover of history. That is evident in the judgments visited on men in their actions. But it is also evident in the ways in which the bad and inadequate can be turned to good ends; in which national and denominational divisions have given rise to a host of viewpoints which form the riches of European cultural history in modern times; in which the Enlightenment contributed to the diminution of confessional hostility; in which a secularized civilization, in conjunction with Marxism, could be making ready the way for a new Christian mission in the world. But God always wishes to use us as his agents and helpers in the world. We must continually search that history in which we are derived from God. We must look into it repeatedly for help in understanding our own situation, and in finding our proper rôle in historical action. We must be aware of its provisional nature but also realize its universal responsibility.

IX The nation and the human race

Almost sixty years after Friedrich Meinecke described the development of the German political consciousness in terms of the contrasting ideas of 'internationalism and the nation-state', it looks as though the debate has become relevant once more, even after all the disasters which have taken place in our century. The idea of the nation has been pronounced dead innumerable times in the recent past, yet today it is visibly reviving. The supra-national principles, which in the years after the war seemed to offer the only rational course for political thought and action, are already being qualified in the name of national values. This may be a sign that post-war Germany is coming to a crossroads in political thought, but in any event it seems necessary for all politically aware citizens to re-examine their ideas and preconceptions about the national and supra-national bases of political action.

What help in this task can we obtain from our inherited Christian tradition? Can we even expect Christian theology to have a contribution to make to this discussion? I believe we can. It is a discussion which, since the time of the early Church, has been closely involved with central elements of the Christian tradition. I deliberately say the Christian tradition and not Protestant or Catholic teaching, because I believe that in the area of political ethics, just as in other theological issues, we must break down the barriers which confine the traditional denominational forms of Christianity. The original power of biblical ideas lives on in the history and tradition of the different Christian churches, and must be released on our time in all its fullness. For this reason I shall not confine myself to the implications of the Lutheran doctrine of the two kingdoms—perhaps better described as the doctrine of the two forms of God's rule, in the world and in the Church. Nor are ideas of natural law sufficient in themselves to provide a basis for a specifically Christian political ethics. Both approaches allow too little scope to specifically Christian ideas. A Christian political ethics should be marked by the expectation of the Kingdom of God, the coming rule of God over the world. Such an approach would at least be very close to the object of Old Testament hope and also to the centre of Jesus' message.

The idea of the Kingdom of God was important in the Early Church as the context for the discussion about whether national or supra-national considerations should have priority in the organization of political life. The first part of this chapter will be devoted to this. The second part will try to pick out the features of our time which make modern internationalism different from the early Christian and medieval ideas of the Kingdom. This section will also consider the connexions between democratic sympathies and internationalism; that is, it will try to bring out the supra-national, human implications of democratic ideas. The third part will deal specifically with the nation and national consciousness from the point of view of an ethics of the Kingdom of God.

1

The period of the official persecution of Christians in the Roman Empire had still not ended when the great Alexandrian theologian Origen, unable and unwilling to go on regarding Augustus' Empire as no more than a product of the Antichrist, set out to remove the negative attitude of Christians towards the Roman state.

Origen applied to Augustus the messianic saying from the seventy-second psalm, 'In his days righteousness flourished and peace abounded'. In Augustus' establishment of his empire, Origen saw the action of divine providence creating the earthly conditions for the universal spread of the Christian faith:

'God prepared the nations for his teaching. He placed them under a single rule, that of the Great King of Rome, and freed them from the illusion that there are many societies, many nationalities, with no connexion between them'. The opponent to whom Origen addressed these words, the pagan philosopher Celsus, had attacked Christian monotheism on the ground that the worship of a single God would bring disorder, since it destroyed the national characteristics which the Roman state had to respect and foster to preserve its unity. Origen replied that national characteristics would disappear anyway on the Last Day with the dawn of the Kingdom of God, and since Augustus' work had already ended the fragmentation of the world into nations it was working in the same direction as the Christian message: that is, towards the Kingdom of God which would bring all nations together.

In the next century Eusebius of Caesarea, a contemporary of the Constantinian settlement, took Origen's idea further. Arguing from the Gospel of Luke (Lk 2.1), he saw the hand of providence in the simultaneous appearance of Christ and the setting up of the Empire by Augustus. According to Eusebius, 'When the Lord and Saviour appeared and simultaneously with his arrival Augustus became the first of the Romans to be Lord of all nationalities, the pluralistic rule of many ended and peace came to the whole world'. For both Eusebius and Origen the ending of national divisions and the ending of polytheism went together, and this is why Eusebius could regard Constantine as completing the work begun by Augustus. Constantine had not only renewed Augustus' Empire; he had also linked the political unity of the state with the uniqueness of the Christian God.

The theological linking of the universal Christian message with the universal political empire of Constantine and his successors has been frequently condemned. It has been felt as almost a want of taste to bring the kingdom of peace promised by the prophets, which was proclaimed as the Kingdom of God, into association with the secular Roman state. Nevertheless we must remember that the promise of God's coming rule of peace over all nations in the Old Testament had a definite political meaning. The promised Kingdom of God was looked for as the

fulfilment and perfection of political systems, of the legal
ordering of human relations. In the Kingdom of God the life of
men in society was to acquire its truly human form. The hope
for the coming of God's Kingdom must never lose this original
political character; if it does it will become lifeless and irrelevant
to real human behaviour. In practice, the opposite has happened. The Christian message has always been a source of political
energy when people have realized the political implications of
the hope for the Kingdom of God. It is true that the Kingdom
of God which Jesus proclaimed is 'not of this world' (Jn 18.36),
but it is the future of this world, and Christians are right to see
even the present world against the background of the future
which has been promised for it. This means that they are justified in looking out in political affairs for provisional signs of that
hope and in working for provisional realizations of it. After all,
what makes Jesus' message unique is its teaching that the coming Kingdom of God, while belonging to the future, is nevertheless already influencing the present. In view of the original
political character of the hope for the Kingdom, that must be
regarded as applying to politics, not just to the private lives of
Christians. And politics in this context will mean the search for
a system of universal peace and justice. What the biblical
promise of God's rule means is that the coming of this system is
ultimately assured.

The theologians of the early Church therefore had thoroughly
good grounds for connecting the Christian hope for the Kingdom of God with the Roman Empire. And modern Christians
have every reason to ask what provisional form the Christian
hope for a system of universal peace and justice could take in the
present state of world affairs. This involves the risk, now as in
the earlier period, that the Christian Gospel will be misused to
glorify the *status quo*. The early Church, in its relations with the
Byzantine court, did not always escape this danger. However,
the danger is removed if we remain humbly aware that any
Christian ordering of life is at best incomplete and can be no
more than a precursor of the final future of the Kingdom of God.
Neither the United States of Europe nor the transformation of
the United Nations into a genuinely supra-national authority

with some supreme sovereign rights would bring about the Kingdom of God on earth in its final form. It may very well be, however, that that is the direction in which we should channel our efforts to create the best possible contemporary embodiment, provisional though it will be, of the promised Kingdom of God. Many of the phrases in which John F. Kennedy described his vision of a peaceful and more just order of human society throughout the world echo the Old Testament promises of a future universal kingdom of peace. For our time, Kennedy's ideas are perhaps the best illustration of a political universalism inspired by Christianity. Nevertheless, as I have said before, I shall not make the mistake of previous periods and think of the establishment of the Kingdom of God as something which could be brought about by human effort. We must remain constantly aware that any 'Christian' order we can create here and now is bound to be provisional. This impermanence is a feature of all 'good works', private as well as public. That is what Christian humility is, a constant awareness of the distance between our own works and the glory of God. An awareness of this distance, however, does not, when rightly understood, weaken our readiness to act. On the contrary, the very realization of the distance between the promised future of the divine Kingdom of peace and the present state of the world can stimulate us to change the present. The hope of God's promised Kingdom of peace can inspire our imagination and will to eradicate the most obvious faults of our world.

2

What has just been said about the current possibilities of a political universalism inspired by Christianity contains the unspoken assumption that the contemporary political form of God's promised Kingdom of peace and justice will not be a world monarchy. For early Christianity a world monarchy was the earthly image of God's rule over the world. In comparison with it, the later claims to divine right on the part of particular kingdoms inevitably appeared as a decline. Only the world monarch could be regarded as the representative of the world-wide rule of God. However, from the theological point of view the idea of monarchic rule contains an intrinsic ambiguity. A monarch inevitably becomes a competitor as well as a representative of God's rule, since he is the supreme earthly authority, and from his decisions there can be no appeal to any other authority. On the other hand, Jesus Christ is the Messiah, the representative to mankind of God's rule, precisely because he did not seek or claim dominion over mankind but gave himself up to death on a cross for the sake of his preaching of God's rule. As a result he has abolished the opposition between rulers and ruled. The opposition is also abolished for Christians because, by faith, baptism and the Lord's Supper, they are united with Christ. Through this union they share in his kingship as well as in his priesthood. Consequently monarchy, at least absolute monarchy with its fundamental distinction between ruler and people, is not wholly compatible with Christianity. As well as a common priesthood, Christians enjoy a common kingship. This idea contains, historically and theoretically, the Christian roots of modern democracy.

Of course modern democracy has other ancient roots besides Christian ones. Ancient Greek democracy was based on the equality and freedom of all full citizens. Stoic philosophers were the first to recognize that every human being, because of his humanity, had a right to freedom and equality. However, the lesson of Greek history seemed to be that democratic constitutions did not endure because the citizens could not produce the necessary public spirit, and it seemed that the only means of preserving a political system was the rule of a single individual. Equality and freedom came to be regarded as features of a regrettably vanished golden age of the human race.

By similar reasoning, Christian theology came to define human freedom and equality as properties of man's original nature which had been lost by the Fall and would only be recovered in the future bliss of the Kingdom of God. Like the Stoics, then, the mainstream of Christian theology regarded freedom and equality as an intrinsic part of human nature, but one which had been lost through the corruption of the human race. In the Christian view, however, freedom and equality were not only associated with a prehistoric golden age, but were part of God's future, which would reveal the equality of all men before God. And there was also in Christian theology a possibility of laying claim to man's future glory here and now, in the present, in virtue of the community of Christians with Christ, the true man. The Christian faith had made it possible to go beyond the mental world of Stoicism in two important respects. Not only had human beings been free and equal before, in a distant past; they would be free and equal again, and not only in a distant future. Even in the present, human beings could make use of their human nature and destiny; their communion with Christ enabled them to raise themselves above the limitations of their present existence and their own weakness.

The universalism of the Christian hope for a political system based on peace and justice which will unite the whole human race has a close connexion with democratic ideas. This connexion is based in the first place on the principles of democracy. Democratic principles have to do with human beings as human beings, with all human beings, and not just with the members of a particular nation. For this reason internationalism is a fundamental element in democratic philosophy. Many pioneers of democracy hoped that democratic institutions would bring different peoples closer together and create a tendency for the human race to become politically more united. We know today that this tendency does not automatically prevail. Democratic states can give way to nationalism, with a resulting xenophobia greater than anything known in the past. The internationalist ideals of democracy need to be connected with the goal of a universal system of peace embracing the whole human race, and in its turn the hope for a system of universal peace contains features which can only reach full development in a society based on freedom and equality. One feature of the hoped for Kingdom of peace, for example, is that it should enable human beings to achieve their full humanity in association with others. In Daniel's vision, the Kingdom of God for which the Old Testament hoped is represented by a human figure, to distinguish the nature of its rule from the rule of violence prevailing in the kingdoms of the world, which were symbolized by animal figures. It has been pointed out already that the rule of Christ ends any rule by force because, through the cross of Jesus and the sacramental communion of believers with him, it totally abolishes any distinction between rulers and ruled. This was why primitive Christianity believed that the perfecting of man's human nature in the kingdom of God made all distinctions of origin and social position unimportant. To this extent Christian theology was quite right to feel a kinship with Stoic ideas of an original freedom and equality between all men. It took over the Stoic ideas and turned them into a promise for the future of the human race.

The Christian adoption of Stoic ideas changes the meaning of freedom and equality, and thereby the basis of democracy. The Stoic view is that freedom and equality are part of our original human nature and that therefore the men and women of the present time, in spite of all the inequalities which have slipped in in the course of history, are essentially equal and equally free, if one can only get behind the distinctions created by society. On the other hand, Christianity does not regard the distinctions which exist between human beings as non-essential in comparison with what they actually have in common. In the Christian view, the distinctions are only negligible in relation to the common vocation of mankind to share in the Kingdom of God. Christianity does not regard human beings as equal and equally free in what they already are, but as called to a freedom and equality before God which does not yet exist but in which we believe. Democratic ideals are easy to attack when they are taken in the Stoic sense of an already existing equality and freedom. This equality is simply an abstraction from all distinctions, not just those of origin and wealth, but also those of gifts and ability, and where this abstract human equality becomes the criterion of political action it is almost impossible to avoid serious injustices, such as the ironing out of all uniqueness or distinctiveness.

The Christian idea of equality is not like this. The Christian idea is not that everyone should be reduced to a mediocrity in which every voice is worth as much as every other. Equality in the Christian sense means that everyone is to be raised to share in the highest human possibilities. This quality has constantly to be created; it never just exists. The power which creates it is that of brotherhood, fraternity. This third of the basic words of modern democracy, which points most clearly to democracy's Christian roots, is all too easily forgotten by the side of freedom and equality. But it is the power of brotherhood, the power of creative love, which alone can unite diversity into community and, with community, produce an equality which did not exist before. Brotherhood must help to ensure that individuals overcome the limitations of their present existence and become free to share in the common human destiny. Brotherhood means that everyone must be given a genuine chance to share in all the goods of society. Abraham Lincoln saw that this was the true meaning of equality. All are not equal, nor can all be treated equally, but everyone can be given a genuine chance to reach equal goals. This idea of Lincoln's, that everyone must be given a chance, shows what it means to talk about an equality which has still to be brought about.

To sum up: the universal idea of the human race, which will have particular force for a Christian ethics of the Kingdom of God, has not just a relevance to 'foreign policy', to the striving for a peaceful organization of the human race which will include all nations. It also has normative force in 'domestic policy', since democratic ideals are concerned with the nature of man. Not that a democratic state can be set up to encompass all mankind immediately. It must develop in the common life and political institutions of one state at a time, within the confines of a limited national territory. For this reason we can no longer avoid the question of the value to be attributed to national communities in an ethics based on God's rule. This is the only context in which a Christian moral philosophy can deal with the nation without losing its Christian character, and this is why I have only come back to the phenomenon of the nation after looking at the democratic idea of the human race. This procedure also makes it much harder to see good theological reasons for the identification of Christianity and nationalism of which history nevertheless shows so many examples.

3

'The nations' always seem to have become direct political partners of the Christian churches either when the Christian hope
for the Kingdom of God could find no appropriate universal
expression in political life or when the idea of the Kingdom of
God had been changed to such an extent that attempts to find a
corresponding political reality ceased. Both these situations
began to affect Western Europe in the fifth and sixth centuries
AD. The universal Roman Empire, or at least its Western half,
collapsed under the impact of the barbarian invasions, and at
the same time the concept of the Kingdom of God was de-
politicized.

The two processes are connected. It was one of the weaknesses
of Byzantine, as later of medieval kingdom theology, that it
regarded the Christian Empire as indestructible because it was
the earthly representative of God's rule. The result was that the
critical function which the Christian hope for the future should
have performed in relation to any actual organization of life
was forgotten. The collapse of the Western Empire made people
even more vividly aware of the temporary and impermanent
nature of even the *imperium Romanum*. As Byzantine theology
increasingly exalted the role of the kingdom, it was a natural
step to abandon any connexion between the hope for the
Kingdom of God and political life. Augustine expressed the
historical experience of his age when he contrasted the Kingdom
of God with secular political systems.

Augustine thus became the first proponent of a two-kingdoms
theory. This early doctrine is illustrative of many later ones.
The difference of the Kingdom of God from any human
political structures is sharply expressed, but the contrast leads
to nothing. It leads to nothing because the separation of the two
domains means that the Kingdom of God is no longer a
critical force able to transcend the limitations of the political
status quo. Augustine, however, did not put the Kingdom of God
totally beyond history. He separated it from politics only to find
it embodied in the Church, which stood immovable in all the
confusion of his time.

The connexion of the Kingdom of God with the Church had far-reaching historical consequences. Firstly, in the early Middle Ages the Church felt itself to be the heir of the Roman Empire and the only universal institution of Christianity. In political terms it saw itself exclusively in relation to the nations. There now developed, as a theory to justify the collaboration of the Church and the political forces within the unity of Christendom, the idea of the 'two powers', the secular and the spiritual. In this theory, the 'secular arm', whose task was to serve the Kingdom of God by preserving peace and justice, no longer needed to be a worldwide state. In its battle against the claims of the medieval empire the Church was able to ally itself with the nations in opposition to the idea of a single secular organization of Christendom. After the collapse of the Empire the Catholic church re-emerged as the only universal authority over the whole of Christianity alongside national particularism, and retained this position into our period.

This is one form of association between the Church and the nation states. Another appears in Luther's two-kingdoms doctrine, or in its consequences. Luther's doctrine also derives from the medieval theory of the two powers, but since for Luther the spiritual power of the Church is no longer a universal institution, there is a particular danger of the Church becoming dependent on local rulers and later on the nation-states.

Luther was in the tradition of the Augustinian two-kingdoms doctrine in the sense that he no longer saw political life against the background of the hope for the Kingdom of God. As a result, he had no sense of the theological importance of the search for the universal political system which might present at least a provisional form of the promised divine Kingdom of peace. Equally, only because of this blindness could he unquestioningly accept the multiplicity of local rulers, the predecessors of the later nation-states, as the normal form of secular authority. However, this was an extremely serious step. There is much to be said for Luther's doctrine of the two kingdoms. It was keenly aware of the difference between the Kingdom of God and political actuality, and of the difference between Church and state. Nor is it true that it encouraged Christians to be simply passive in their attitude to political authorities. Nevertheless, the difference between the Kingdom of God and everyday politics could no longer, in Luther's theory, produce any power to change day-to-day situations. Instead, the political sphere was left clear for the action of powers which were not committed to Christian aims, as the Christian Empire by definition had been. There were, it is true, Christian-inspired rulers, but the vital interests of the petty states of the sixteenth century, and still more those of the later nation-states, had little to do with Christian ideas or aims. This is the weakness of Luther's two-kingdoms doctrine.

There is no need to examine in detail here the ways in which the political interests of the new states diverged from Christian ideas and aims. What we must examine next is the contradiction between Christianity and modern nationalism, even though this does not exhaust all that a Christian political philosophy could say about the nation.

The raising of the nation in modern times to the status of a model for political action stands in clear opposition to the supra-national traditions of Christianity and the source of those traditions, the Christian hope of the Kingdom of God for all men. A particularly clear indication of this is the way in which nationalism has developed its identity by attaching itself to biblical ideas. This process has involved the distortion of the biblical ideas, and has gone in some cases as far as the deification of the nation. For example, the idea of the Chosen People was applied to modern nations like England and Germany to give their development the aura of a religious mission. The tendency to think of one's own people as chosen by analogy with ancient Israel in fact ignores the uniqueness of Israel in salvation history to which its title, God's Chosen People, points. Furthermore, the purpose of choosing this people was to win the whole human race for the God of Israel. In Jesus Christ and the universal Christian mission this purpose was in essence achieved, in the sense that there then took place a transition from the choice of only one people to the call to all mankind to share the Christian salvation. From this point on the idea of the Chosen People is a step backwards from the Christian movement towards the whole human race. For this reason the secular use of the idea in nationalism must be declared anti-Christian.

It was no accident that the national idea helped to drive Christian motives out of the process of political decision-making in modern times. A world in which national interests dominate diplomacy and politics is one which has no room for the Christian expectation of a Kingdom of God which will be a system of justice and peace for the whole human race. The Christian churches did not see sufficiently clearly that these developments inevitably led political life away from the spirit of Christianity, and underestimated their importance. They never, even in Germany, joined totally in the cult of nationalism, but they were unable to break out of it. They were unable to open it up to wider political aims and connect it with the universal perspective of Christian hope. Under the shadow of the two-powers theory, the churches compromised with nationalism, when it was their vocation, if anyone's, to oppose a development which led the nations of Europe to tear each other to pieces in the name of national fantasies.

It must not be said that this destruction was merely the result of exaggerations of the idea of the nation which could have been avoided. Views of this sort have recently become widespread, but they minimize the real problem. When the nation becomes the cornerstone of political philosophy, a battle for leadership is in the long run inevitable. The Romantic forerunners of German nationalism did not preach chauvinism. They believed in harmonious co-existence between nations. Nonetheless their ideas led to competition in power politics as in culture, and to battles for supremacy. The harmonious co-existence of peoples which was the ideal of Herder and Schleiermacher is only possible in the long term within a framework of wider aims and supra-national institutions.

Of course a Christian political philosophy would not have to deny the nation any significance for political theory or activity. National ties resulting from a shared language, a shared culture, a shared historical experience or the combination of all these— these are beyond question historical facts which require attention and which no one can simply ignore. It is important to be clear about their significance. The closest analogy which comes to mind with the unity of a nation is the idea of the community within the family, though the family has been less affected by historical changes than the nation. In the moral theology of the last century the nation and the family were often regarded as part of the 'order of creation', as divine institutions. This idea is complex. In the first place it is a theological formulation of the observation that nations exist in fact and that every man or woman is part of some nation. As well as this, however, the idea of divine institution also implies obligations on the part of the individual towards the nation or the family. This is where the difficulties appear. There is nothing in the idea of the order of creation to connect the nation with specifically Christian ideas, and this alone makes it suspicious that references to the nation as a divine institution attempt to go beyond the acknowledgment of the factual existence of nations to derive particular obligations on the part of their members from that mere existence. The mere existence of a nation certainly does not prove that the preservation of national characteristics is part of God's will. The characteristics and the size of nations have undergone many changes in the course of history. Some nations have disappeared and others have come into being. The mere fact of the existence of a national unit does not entail any 'imperative of loyalty' for the members of a nation. The use of the concept of the order of creation to explain the fact of national cohesion remains, therefore, questionable, particularly as it has proved so easy for nationalists to misuse.

The fact that the people of a nation are bound together by national ties acquires a different significance when considered against the background of the Christian hope for the coming of the Kingdom of God. The union of all men in a kingdom of peace and justice cannot be brought about by directly forcing individuals throughout the world into association. It will only come about as an association of a number of large groups which in turn consist of unions of smaller groups. The development and encouragement of a sense of common identity wherever a basis for it exists is the only way to build larger political units. Not individuals in isolation, but the groups they constitute can join to form larger associations This is the positive significance of national identity; it is an inevitable stage in the development of the greater unity of mankind. Implicit in this is the criterion which puts a limit on national egotism.

Against this background we can understand the justice of the demand for nation-states which inspired the nationalist movements of the last century. Shared national characteristics are not sufficient to justify the demand, however, and part of its force derives from the claim to political self-determination, which is based on human dignity, the idea that men are meant to be free and equal. It should also be noted that the demand for the nation-state cannot have the absolute character which was claimed for it in the past. A state including many nationalities, such as the old Austria-Hungary, may not under all circumstances be a bad thing. This idea will not be difficult to accept for those who regard the work of forming political communities as one which in any case goes beyond the frontiers of their own nation.

Seeing national identity as a stage in the progress towards the greater unity of the human race allows for the cultivation of national characteristics, a particular language, culture and way of life. A multiplicity of mutually complementary characteristics will be a stronger unifying factor than uniformity in a wider grouping. However, the cultivation of specific characteristics will only be justified to the extent that it contributes to the life of the wider group.

In particular, all encouragement of national characteristics must be subordinated to the task of building a supra-national system of justice and peace. We know to our cost that international harmony is not a spontaneous growth. The development of supra-national institutions also ought to start with limited groups, and build on common elements in history and culture, and shared political and economic tasks. The best example of such steps towards unity in our period is perhaps the process of European integration, though such unions of nations should yet again look beyond their frontiers to the ideal of a just and peaceful order which would eventually embrace the whole human race, not just our friends in the world, but our current opponents. The sequence of particular amalgamations outlined above, which has to begin in the internal political life of each nation and which has a place for the community of the nation, is also directed to the universal political aim of a peaceful order including the whole of mankind. Because of its connexion with the biblical hope for the Kingdom of God, this idea must be the norm of any Christian political philosophy. Used as a norm, it implies, for example, that the idea of a united Europe will only acquire its full moral force if this Europe does not shut itself off from the rest of the world.

A united Europe will also have to be able to display the humanity of its people in its culture and democratic structures in such a way that it exercises an attraction on the rest of mankind. With regard to the national problems of Germany, our criterion of the biblical hope for the Kingdom of God implies that national interests should not be treated as ends in themselves, but pursued in a context of wider goals, the first of which is European unity. This connexion with the wider political goals of European unity and world peace determines the boundary between the legitimate fostering of national ties and nationalist excesses.

At this point I shall be a little more specific. No German political programme can abandon the attempt to find a new political expression of national ties with the millions of German men and women on the other side of the Elbe, in the German Democratic Republic. The form of this political association must be the result of a free decision of the whole German people. This is a self-evident implication of the idea of human dignity, of the human vocation to freedom and equality, and it is a demand which will acquire increasing force the more convincingly this human vocation is displayed in the Federal Republic of Germany. On the other hand, the demand for the restoration of the 1937 frontiers seems to me defensible today only in terms of a fairly abstract idea of national rights. Is the Polish population which today lives on the other side of the Oder and the Neisse to be transplanted yet again? If so, where to? Must we wait for the Soviet Union to give Poland back its old eastern territories? These are obviously totally unreal hopes, and the survival of such aspirations among sections of the Federal German population should no longer receive official encouragement. This remark is also relevant to the national interest. An obstinate insistence on the unattainable may very well result in throwing away for some time what might have been obtained by various other approaches—I mean political union with the Germans living across the Elbe. Without an agreement with East European neighbours, in particular with the Poles, this urgent national desire can have very little chance of satisfaction. We are constantly being told that all territorial settlements must wait for a peace treaty. But does anyone really maintain that a peace treaty is still likely after twenty years? Isn't a peace treaty becoming less necessary year by year? What policies towards Eastern Europe will show in the long run is how far German policy is prepared to accommodate national desires within a wider European perspective and subordinate them to the demands of humanity. Will Germans instead, in the name of some national principles, shut their eyes for all time to the situation created by the result of the war, which to all human estimation is hardly likely to alter? It may not always be possible at the moment for those who hold political office in Federal Germany to discuss this question openly. If so, it is the duty of all other citizens to talk about it. Only through such discussion can an atmosphere be created in which a German government will one day have the freedom to take appropriate action.

Germans are constantly being told that they lack a sense of national identity. The observation is very true, but the lack is the result of a lack of clarity in the present political situation. A German patriotism free from nationalist exaggeration can only develop when West Germans decide to stop repressing from their political consciousness the result of the War in the eastern German State. Only then can a German once more pronounce the word 'Fatherland' without worrying whether he is embarking on a political adventure with incalculable consequences. Even then, however, patriotism must never again become the highest virtue in our political thought and practice. The German contribution to a more secure system of world peace in the future should be to avoid being swayed by the pressures of day-to-day politics and hold fast to the goal of European unity, a unity which must involve more than a *Europe des patries*. A political policy which works for this universal goal contributes not only to the realization of the universal human vocation to harmonious co-existence, but also to educating the citizens of an individual country for true freedom and equality. Such a policy may well claim to be sustained from the deepest roots of the Christian tradition, while at the same time it is the policy most likely to satisfy the national needs of the German people.

X Christian morality and political issues

Christian involvement with contemporary issues, especially political issues, is a new phenomenon. It seems sometimes to depend more on a compulsion to engage in political activity than on a clear understanding of means and ends. It is now realized that the individualism of a wholly private piety and traditional Christian authoritarian morality consciously or unconsciously help to maintain existing structures of domination, and certainly did so in the past. In an atmosphere of widespread questioning of all existing authority structures, that has produced a tendency for Christians to ally with radical political opposition groups, without being sufficiently clear about the implications of the alternative social and political models such opposition is supposed to, and does in fact, support. The supporters of this opposition, who today like to call themselves revolutionaries because they distrust all fixed rules of opposition, make two claims. They say they will put an end to attacks on Christian conservatism as supporting inhuman forms of authority. They also claim that they can reveal a new relevance of Christianity.

A danger of the second claim is that political commitment may become a substitute for relevance to our sense of reality and our behaviour which is otherwise found lacking in Christian faith. Political activity cannot really replace the sense of reality given by faith and its practice in everyday life. There is a new eagerness among Christians to take a critical part in political life, but it may very well be killed off by disillusionment and frustration unless serious theological consideration is given to the association between Christian belief and political action and the

problems it raises. Christian slogans must not be allowed to
become, under a new banner, window-dressings for views and
positions reached on different grounds.

1

Even those who think Christians have to play a critical part in
political life, and they especially, must face the weight of the
views which so far in the Christian tradition have discouraged
such a position. No discussion of this subject can avoid the fact
that in the course of its history Christianity has in the main held
back from involvement in economic and political issues in 'the
world'. Today we are particularly sensitive to the weakness of
such a position, since inevitably it favours the existing power-
structures. On the other hand, aloofness from the central
preoccupations of the human world (that is, economics and
politics) is ineradicably touched with the autonomy of Christian
and 'religious' preoccupations in regard to mundane things and
objects of concern to worldly existence. That that very aloofness helps to preserve human dignity; ultimately, perhaps, that
is Christianity's most important contribution, though one too
easily robbed of credibility by other aspects of Christian
behaviour.

Let me preface my remarks with a text which is a classic
source for the traditional Christian attitude. The Gospel of
John makes Jesus say to Pilate: 'My kingship is not from this
world' (Jn 18.36). The Johannine Jesus does not say that his
kingship is not effective *in* this world, but points to its origin,
which is different from that of human power-seeking. Pilate's
question, however, was whether Jesus was in the politically
suspect sense 'King of the Jews'; that is to say, potentially at
least, an agitator against Roman rule in Palestine. Jesus'
answer is that his kingdom, the kingdom of 'truth', does not
take the form of political power. The point of the saying expresses something of the authentic meaning of Jesus' message about
the Kingdom of God, but in a very specific application which
is slightly swamped by the generality of the statement.

Jesus' rejection of the political messianism of his people and its extension in political revolt against Roman rule did not imply that the rule of God which he preached was totally and in principle neutral on all political issues. There is no doubt that the Johannine Christ's words to Pilate, 'My kingship is not from this world', have been taken in this more general sense. They have been used to justify a doctrine of the two kingdoms which makes the religious and political domains mutually autonomous or admits their connexion only in the person of a Christian, who belongs to both worlds. This sort of generalized interpretation is not part of the context of the Johannine saying, though it is an extension of one of its strands. A separation of religious and political elements is however incompatible with Old Testament Judaism's hope in the rule of God, which was also central to Jesus' message. Jesus was reserved towards the political messianism of the Zealots, most probably because he expected the coming of God's rule as an act of God and not as a result of human action, but it has very little to do with an apolitical conception of God's rule as such. However, this does not alter the fact that, whereas the rule of God affects all areas of life, its emergence in Jesus' own preaching has no particular political emphasis.

Because of this, theological attempts to justify critical political activity by Christians have always found more abundant and evident support in the Old Testament, and especially in its prophetic writings. Yahweh's action in history, which was the basis of Israel's religion, always had a political character. It was political, not in the narrow sense of belonging to a special area of human activity, but in the broad sense of being concerned with the general conditions of the existence of a human community, a nation, in contact with the rest of mankind. The saving gift of the Land, the legal system, the institution of the holy war, the mysterious figures of the Judges of Israel's prehistory, and finally the founding of the kingdom with the choice of David and Zion; all those were strongly political events and facts. The political nature of Israelite religion had of course many parallels in other early cultures, where the close association of religion and political life was a characteristic feature.

What is striking about Israel is the growing importance of a religiously motivated political criticism. This prophetic critique gave expression to an idea of the transcendence of the God of Israel in relation to his people which became vital to the survival of Israel's religion in the later monarchy. This transcendence made not only the actions of the Israelites and their kings, but increasingly the whole of contemporary world history, the object of prophetic judgments.

Surely this prophetic activity provides a suitable model for modern political preaching? Unfortunately, anyone who carefully examines the question and weighs the arguments and counter-arguments will most probably come to the opposite conclusion, not only because of the difference between our world and that of ancient Israel, but also on specifically theological grounds.

For the religion of ancient Israel, the archaic unity of all areas of life in religion was still intact. In contrast the modern view of life is marked by processes in which human activity, in its highly developed ramifications, is separated from traditional religious ties and becomes independent of them. The heteronomy of a world in which existence was enclosed within a sacral sphere has been replaced by an autonomy of our attitude to the natural world and our ordering of social relations among human beings. One result of this is that belief in he divine control of the course of history can no longer support criticism of political conditions as directly as it could for Israel's prophets. When sermons or ecclesiastical statements today imitate the prophetic attitude and relate God's action in history to specific political situations they often seem to mix incompatible forms of knowledge and reasoning, secular knowledge and religious language.

If theological formulas from the past retain validity in political criticism, it is usually in an interpretative rather than an argumentative mode. Arguments based on divine judgment, or even on the authority of a special divine saying, are not a sufficient basis for a convincing critique of a contemporary political situation. Even when political criticism from theologians adopting a prophetic stance has made an impact in our time, its effectiveness has owed less to its reliance on divine authority than to its power to clarify the intricacies of political situations—sometimes in combination with the moral authority of the critic, as in the case of Martin Niemöller.

Whereas ancient prophecy's political criticism, while it may have made use of political understanding in the modern sense, could bring Israel's religious traditions into a detailed analysis of specific situations, modern political criticism must draw its arguments entirely from secular knowledge. A question inevitably arises about this knowledge. It does not operate as a value-free skill, least of all in a left-wing attack on the *status quo*. It is natural to ask what vision prompts and gives force to its analysis. It makes a difference whether a political situation is examined and assessed in terms of nationalist convictions, democratic pluralism, Marxist bias, or a Christian theology of history. Different underlying philosophies will select and emphasize different aspects. This does not mean that a political issue should be argued in philosophical terms, rather than in terms of what the philosophy reveals. The observations are a measure of the vision that inspires them. It is only in the uncovering of the roots of a particular situational analysis, the tracing of the underlying perspectives and their classification in terms of their ultimate implications, that theological categories can have a rational function.

At this point a question arises about the basis of the theological perspective which can give rise to political criticism. Here again ancient prophecy cannot be a direct model. A Christian's relationship to Old Testament prophecy comes through Jesus, and he seems to have regarded himself as the end of prophecy: 'All the prophets and the law prophesied until John' (Mt 11.13). That is to say: not only does their prophecy point to John, the new Elijah, but John, as the new Elijah, was the ultimate embodiment of prophetic activity, a prophet and as the last prophet 'more than a prophet' (Mt 11.9). If these sayings go back to Jesus, it means that he did not regard himself as a prophet. His coming is the dawn of that coming of God foretold by prophecy. Because the ultimate object of all prophetic language, the coming of God to rule, is now taking place in Jesus, his coming is the end of prophecy. Christianity cannot

retreat from this point. In Christian theology prophetic proclamation must be replaced by an interpretation of what has
now become history through Jesus. On the other hand, what
became a historical event in Jesus is the final coming of the rule
of God which was announced by the prophets, and consequently Jesus is not the end of prophecy in the sense that it has
now been disproved, but in the sense that in him its fulfilment has
taken place. This aspect must also be part of the Christian assess-
ment of the prophetic attitude to history, the prophets' political
criticism.

At the same time it must not be forgotten that although the
end of history has dawned with the presence of God's rule in the
appearance and end of Jesus, for the rest of the world it is still
to come. For the world it is still future. In this sense John's
gospel is quite right to contrast the Kingdom of Christ—the
Kingdom of God—with the kingdoms of the world. The future
character of God's rule allows the world around us to be completely secular; though since it is the future of this world, and
not a different one, it has begun to act on it in the message and
history of Jesus Christ and so has already come in him. Christian
preaching of what happened in Jesus is therefore addressed to a
world which has been freed from religious restrictions and has
become secular; its task is to make the world aware of its own
future in the light of God's future, which also means aware of its
potential and need for change.

The most important factor in interpreting the human, and
especially the political, relevance of the message of Christ is the
way the eschatological meaning of the message and history of
Jesus is interpreted: that is, the way in which the end of history
is regarded as having come in Christ. If the end of history is taken
to mean that history simply stops, this must entail in Christian
spirituality a resolute withdrawal from the concerns of this
world; especially from its social, economic and political
problems. In that case, the natural institutional form of Christian spirituality in society will be either private activity or
purely religious communities. If, on the other hand, the end of
the world and its history which has come in Jesus is viewed
positively as the fulfilment of the world and history, by analogy

with the human resurrection expected as part of this end, in a world purified by God's judgment and transfigured by his presence, Christian spirituality will be intent on transforming every aspect of the present and bringing it to fulfilment. It is characteristic of the Christian religion that it no longer looks to that end as simply in the future, but sees it as a force acting on the present and thereby transforming it, just as it can be seen to have acted in Jesus' life and is believed to act in the lives of Christians.

By faith we lay hold of the reality of God in Jesus, and that reality has power to transform our lives here and now. The first Christians, however, associated that reality and that power almost exclusively with individual conduct. This is striking in Paul, as when he says in the Epistle to the Romans that the baptized should now yield their members 'to righteousness for sanctification' (Rom 6.19). There is no parallel in the social institutions of public life to the individual 'renewal of the mind' of Rom 12.2. Later doctrines of the two kingdoms reinforced this one-sided interpretation of the implications of Christian faith for individual conduct by restricting sanctification to this area, a restriction which does not adequately represent the scope of Jesus' message of the imminence of the rule of God. There are two main reasons for primitive Christianity's failure to go beyond individual conduct in its analysis of the transformation and renewal of life here and now as a result of the presence of God's rule in Christ. The first is the low social status of the first Christians; and the second their imminent expectation of the end. They expected the end of the existing world to come rapidly, since it seemed to have begun with the raising of Christ, and there was no time left for institutional reforms. If we take account of these two specific factors in the situation of the early Christians, we must regard the New Testament's general calls for peace and obedience, which certainly represent 'a typical servile ethic', as in fact indicative (and Hans von Campenhausen argues thus) of a fundamentally positive attitude to social responsibilities. However, the merely passive servile ethic of the New Testament should not be misinterpreted as permanently binding on all Christian activity. It was the product of the status of the first Christians, which denied them any active political responsibility, and was consequently bound to change as soon as the politically active became Christians or Christians gained political office. As, with the fading of the initial expectation of a rapid end to things, Christians began to get used to the idea that this world might last for some time, change in social structures as a form of present sharing in God's rule gradually became a permissible topic.

Significantly for the future, little came of this. It is true that Christianity, particularly after the Constantinian settlement, came to terms with the social and political responsibilities that now fell to Christians. And it cannot be said that Christianity took over the existing social and political conditions and institutions without any modification. Nevertheless, as with the assimilation by Christians of philosophical theology, where pre-Christian conditions could be adapted to Christianity they were not probed too deeply. The Emperor and his power were no longer an image of the unconquered Sun, but the earthly manifestation of Christ the King of Heaven. This was made theologically possible by the familiarity in late prophecy and apocalyptic of the idea that the kingdoms of the world were representatives of the rule of Yahweh. The Christian interpretation of the imperial office certainly did more than change the ideological label. The once divine Emperor was now a man in need of redemption by Christ in exactly the same way as his subjects, and he could only share in redemption through the mediation of the Church. The status and authority this gave the Church in the person of its bishops *vis à vis* the Emperor as early as the Byzantine Empire had no counterpart in pre-Christian Rome. The change also contained a variety of important implications, not least the right of the people of Byzantium to rebel against an Emperor who departed from orthodoxy.

However, the change in power structures did not go deep enough. During the Christianization of the Roman Empire, and even later during the whole period when Christendom was united in religion and politically powerful, many of the implications of God's rule in the work and history of Christ remained without serious consequences. Jesus had practised God's rule as love. In God's name he had invited the subjects of that rule, and even rebels against it, to eat with him. He identified with them, served them, and by associating with them gave them a share in his rule; in other words, he abolished the distinction between rulers and ruled. He showed that God's rule means, paradoxically, the cancellation of the distinction between rulers and ruled, and so, in a sense, the abolition of all rule. But in Christendom this significance of divine rule was not understood. Instead it came to be regarded as an indestructible divine ordinance that the King of Heaven should be represented on earth by the monarch or later by the Pope, who now gave himself rather than the Emperor the title 'Vicar of Christ'. This theory of representation was later developed into a complete hierarchy of orders.

The idea of monarchy as an image of divine rule is a fundamental form of the concept of order. This concept was characteristic of Christianity's appropriation and interpretation of the social structures it inherited from the ancient world, and has remained influential down to our own time. 'Order' in this sense means not just a way of organizing human relations within society which is in principle open to change, but a divinely instituted, and therefore sacred and untouchable, form of human relations. Another form of the concept of order grew out of the medieval two-powers theory, the origin of which in the early Church has already been mentioned. The limitation of the secular state by a spiritual power had an undoubted tendency to transfer to the spiritual power features of secular rule, notably the use of force, but at the same time it was an incentive to interpret the spiritual power in genuinely spiritual terms and so, in an extension of Augustinian ideas, as a contemporary form of the rule of Christ. The great merit of Luther's doctrine of the two forms of government is that it sharpened the awareness of this spiritual character of the rule of Christ in the face of all the distortions of clerical power. Luther did this by bringing the legacy of the medieval movement for spiritual reform into his version of the two-powers theory, but the price of this was the identification of the sphere of Christ's rule as the Church. Political power now almost totally lost the connexion with the rule of Christ, or the rule of God present in Christ, which it had retained in the primitive Christian and medieval idea of the kingdom. Instead it was subordinated to the task of sustaining human life, whose connexion with Christ and the order of redemption was only indirect. A Christian spirit was also supposed to influence individual Christians in secular positions, but it had no effect on the understanding of those offices.

This secularization of worldly rule had the unintended effect of accelerating the complete emancipation of political power, first in the principalities and later in the absolutist nation-states. It is here that the ambivalence of the doctrine of the two forms of government appears. In the context of our discussion, however, the main point of interest is that in spite of all differences, just like the idea of the Christian (originally the imperial) monarchy, it is a model of an 'order' of political and social life. Here again the power structure of that life remained intact; indeed, it was reinforced to meet any influence for change deriving from the idea of the rule of Christ, the character of which as the abolition of all rule Luther had seen quite clearly. The only alternative to making the political sphere independent of the order of redemption he would seem to have considered was an attempt to present the rule of Christ itself as a system of political organization— on the part of the 'fanatics' and, in a more refined form, in a worldly papacy. Luther rightly rejected both as distortions of the spiritual meaning of the rule of Christ and of the temporary nature of all secular institutions.

2

The real mistake is in the concept of order itself. Christian ethics should not be dominated by an order which has to be preserved, but by the idea of transformations. This has been the case as regards individual conduct, where repentance, change of attitude, renewal of the mind and sanctification have been the substance of Christian ethics since the time of the early Church; but this view of things did not influence attitudes to social structures until much later, and then only in a piecemeal way. Certainly society cannot be organized definitively as the sphere of Christ's rule; but the same is true of the life of the individual Christian. Just as a Christian, while remaining the Old Man, tries to let himself be increasingly permeated by the reality of the New Man he has met in faith, so a Christian movement should be felt in social life. It will not be able to eliminate the distinctions between rulers and ruled, or the conflicts between power structures, from one day to the next, but it can prepare the way for changes in existing conditions.

It was in this spirit that seventeenth-century English and American Christians ventured to apply their equality before God and their freedom in Christ to the organization of their political affairs. As sharers in the kingship and priesthood of Christ, they claimed the right to organize their secular society themselves instead of letting this remain the privilege of a ruler acting alone in God's place. This is not the place to discuss the structures and the problems to which this development gave rise in modern constitutional and democratic States, but it is important to notice that it represents the decisive move to a Christian ethics of transformations which now includes public life.

The way in which the change came about is also important. Out of religious awareness, faith in Christ, a vision of relationships between human beings arose which can be applied here and now in practical action. It can be used to change existing institutions, even though it may not bring about the definitive realization of a fraternal society in which men live in freedom and equality. On the contrary, localized changes in existing conditions are constantly needed to reveal human freedom and equality more completely. In a given situation particular features demand attention as particularly intolerable obstacles to human freedom and equality. Changing them means that another step is taken towards humanizing the world—the next one, the one needed now; but subsequently we transfer our attention to other features, which in turn seem to embody all that separates human beings from the attainment of their destiny.

In an ethics of change man and his social environment are seen as part of a process. Man is on a path from what he actually is to what he potentially is and is destined to be. The current

historical situation and the course of history are not separate
elements in this approach. Theology here does not confront
profane life as an alien sphere calling for technical knowledge,
but seeks to change existing conditions. The present situation
forms part of the ethical analysis by showing where change can
and should take place. The subsequent phases of the process
show how far the attempts at change have succeeded or failed
to humanize the situation. If they fail, the causes of the failure
must be discovered, and ways found to eliminate them. Even if
they succeed, new difficulties and needs appear, although that
does not mean that the social action of Christians has always to
start again from the beginning. Like their individual sanctification, it is part of a history of attempts to create a Christian
existence, and it only progresses by reflection on this in a process
of learning from its own historical experience.

In an ethics of change the course of history and God's action
in history are no longer seen as something which just happens to
human beings, which they must accept passively, but as the
sphere of human action. God is not seen as acting in competition
with man in history, but through human action, both in its
success and in its failure. He is the power of a substantial future,
by which human action is inspired when it opens itself to its
human destiny and on which it comes to grief when it tries to
ignore that destiny. Human destiny, however, is not something
we can just decide. In order to recognize it and approximate
to it, we have to depend on the emergence of a spirit which opens
the eyes of individuals to their destiny and brings them together
to achieve it. This spirit is not under our control, but we can
easily ignore it and thus miss the point of our existence. One of
theology's ways of presenting this fact is its use of the traditional
terminology of the grace, patience or judgment of God—indeed,
rightly understood, th' dimension of historical experience can
only be adequately described in these categories. In this sense,
the great words of the theology of history may well be irreplace-
able and not interchangeable. Nevertheless the conclusion of
my discussion on prophetic language remains true. The vener-
able categories of God's grace, patience or judgment are only
valid or intelligible as interpretations of human situations.

They do not refer directly to a special state of affairs which can only be interpreted by a special theological technique but can be used as premisses in an empirical argument.

An extreme case of an ethics of social transformations is revolution, understood as a fundamental change in social organization. An ethics of change will treat this problem quite differently from one based on orders. An ethics of the second type will permit wars in defence of an existing divinely-willed order but categorically reject the overthrow of that order, while an ethics based on the transformation of human society in the direction of greater human dignity will tend to take the opposite view. Revolution cannot be ruled out as the ultimate implication of the process of transforming society, whereas the causes of war will have to be abolished by a common effort of all nations. This is regarded as possible once adequate machinery is set up for changing the relationships of societies with one another, and their internal structures. It is typical of modern forms of government such as the constitutional state or a democracy that the constitutional structure already allows for the possibility of changes and provides machinery for it. It is therefore likely that the need for revolutionary upheavals will be less often felt in such societies than in rigid societies based on reverence for institutions or authoritarian rule. Where however the legal institutions of constitutional and democratic states are not capable of allowing social change, or are prevented from functioning by the manipulations of powerful groups, then, even in conditions of formal democracy, revolution (that is, a fundamental alteration of social organization, without, or if necessary with, violence) can be morally justified; in some circumstances it is a duty.

The change in the traditionally reserved Christian attitude to political questions is itself an example of the application of an ethics of social transformations. We must now look, finally, at the social situation which generally prevented the development of such a Christian attitude in the post-Reformation period and in particular held back any corresponding political activity.

In the post-Reformation period the theological trend towards the separation of religion and politics, which originated in the medieval two-powers theory, combined with a social process: the privatization of religious belief in modern constitutions. The fact that in this period religion was regarded as a private matter is the source of a vigorous prejudice against the intervention of religious aims and arguments in political discussion and action. The relegation of religion to the private sphere forced even the Roman Catholic Church in this period to adopt a more cautious attitude to political affairs. Not only did the restriction of religion to the private sphere limit Christian influence on political institutions; it contributed to the impression that religion was simply the concern of the individual, and of his own subjective decision, without any generally binding truth.

To appreciate the way in which adherence to Christianity became a private matter in the post-Reformation period, we must remember that historically it was a consequence of the denominational divisions and the religious wars of the sixteenth and seventeenth centuries. The conflict between different forms of religion, each opposing the other with authoritarian exclusiveness, made it impossible, in areas in which religious uniformity could no longer be imposed, to base the political unity of the state on religion, as had before been considered natural. If political unity was not to be endangered, the state had to become free and relegate religious differences to the sphere of its citizens' private affairs.

The separation of state and religion was and is inevitable as a reaction to any authoritarian form of Christianity which proclaims itself as the only true form without reference to rational argument and is therefore fundamentally intolerant of other faiths. In the sixteenth century Christianity was not able to solve the problem of tolerance, or the reasons for tolerance, in terms of its own Christian ideas because the various denominational positions were unable to recognize the relative and transitory nature of their theological knowledge in comparison with the reality of the God revealed in Christ. Consequently tolerance, at least in civil life, had to be secured by banishing religion to the private sphere.

The separation of state and Church was historically necessary, and remains necessary today in the face of any form of Christianity which is authoritarian and not automatically pluralistic. We must therefore consider the problems which have resulted from this separation for the churches and for society.

The separation of the Christian denominations from the state means that there is no longer any agreement about the moral basis of the unity of society. This is the central concern of the sociology of religion. In the sociology of religion, religion is defined as what provides the basis for a society's moral unity, in particular the unity of its sense of values. The relegation of the Christian faith to the private sphere does not mean that political life as such has become neutral as regards religion, but that in the domain of politics the sociological function of religion has been taken over by outlooks other than those represented by the Christian denominations. In the constitutional states of the modern period this was initially, and remains officially today (as in the Basic Law of the Federal Republic of Germany), a more or less watered-down general Christian theism. This is also the only visible form of Christianity, as opposed to its denominationally divided organizational forms.

As early as the constitutions of the seventeenth and eighteenth centuries, however, this general Christian theism was largely replaced by a belief in the state (absolutism), or by a nationalism which was later adopted by other ideologies. It has often been claimed, with some truth, that in present-day western society, with its hostility to ideology, the lowest common denominator which unites individuals is private interest and the creation of a private life. Everything else—religion, art, and now increasingly science—is optional, part of the range of consumer goods. Such a reduction of the general idea of common humanity to the principle of private interest is intolerable, and this would seem to be the underlying cause of present-day unrest among young people and the renewed attraction of socialist ideas which might have been thought to have been devalued by Stalinism.

If, ultimately, the separation of state and religion is impossible in state and public life, the restriction of religious truth to the private domain is also essentially intolerable to Christianity. What gives Christianity its energy is its proclamation of the revelation of the one God of all men; it thereby makes a claim which binds all men and tends to join them together. The restriction of Christianity to the subjective freedom of the private breaks this bond, and the sense of the irrelevance of the Christian faith which has been growing in recent decades may well have a close connexion with this privatization.

Are there ways out of this situation which at the same time respect essential elements of the separation of Church and state which have to be preserved? It is clear at any rate that any new discussion of the relationship between Christianity and society will have to be conducted with a Christianity which is supra-denominational and no longer authoritarian. This gives the ecumenical movement direct relevance to the question of the social, public rôle of Christianity. If Christians succeed in solving the problems of their own pluralism, they may be able to produce a model combining pluralism and the widest moral unity which will also be valid for political life.

Since the Reformation, the dichotomy of religion and politics has become a widespread and securely established prejudice. It can only be broken down if its sociological premiss, that religion is a private matter, is rejected. That will be possible only if Christianity can emerge from the authoritarian life and thought patterns that still affect the various denominations. Current attempts to develop a political theology and to define the public responsibilities of Christians will find a wider hearing if they are more prepared than now to forsake denominational claims, and if the Christian perspective enables them to articulate the demands of humanity in political discussion.